3

TRUMPET AT FULL MOON

TRUMPET AT FULL MOON

An Introduction to Christian Spirituality as Diverse Practice

W. PAUL JONES

Westminster/John Knox Press
Louisville, Kentucky

Book design by Gene Harris

First edition

Published by Westminster/John Knox Press
Louisville, Kentucky

This book is printed on acid-free paper that meets the American National Standards Institute Z39.48 standard. ∞

PRINTED IN THE UNITED STATES OF AMERICA

9 8 7 6 5 4 3 2 1

Library of Congress Cataloging-in-Publication Data

Jones, W. Paul.
    Trumpet at full moon : an introduction to Christian spirituality as diverse practice / W. Paul Jones. — 1st ed.
        p.   cm.
    Includes bibliographical references.
    ISBN 0-664-25231-1
    1. Spirituality.   2. Meditations.   3. Spiritual exercises.
I. Title.
BV4501.2.J663 1992   91-37843
248—dc20

To my daughters
Kathy, Amy, Wendy, Suzanne, Elise
who have taught me
that uniqueness need not
be exclusive

Sing aloud to God . . . ;
   shout for joy . . . .
Raise a song . . . .
Blow the trumpet at the new moon,
   at the full moon, on our feast day.

                —Psalm 81:1–3

For the joy of ear and eye,
   For the heart and mind's delight,
For the mystic harmony
   Linking sense to sound and sight.

—From "For the Beauty of the Earth"
   Folliot S. Pierpoint (1835–1917)

For from [God] and through [God]
and to [God] are all things.

                —Romans 11:36

Contents

A Prelude

Talk of spirituality appears frequently now, and in the strangest places. But the more one reads, the more one is pushed to ask the central question: "What on earth is it?" Whatever answer is forthcoming, sooner or later one encounters the conflict between two delightfully different groups. On the one hand, there are the *professional theologians*, of which I am one. We should *know* what spirituality is. But we are notorious for having little to do with practicing it. On the other hand, there are those who appear by their practices to *be* spiritual. Yet many of these lack a theological sophistication sufficient to keep the enterprise from having an aura of naïveté or escapism.

This book is birthed within that strange tension between theoreticians and practitioners. In fact, I must confess that it had its inception in professional embarrassment. I could not find an authentic introduction to spirituality that was theologically sound yet understandable, while at the same time providing broad experiential options that were informed by the full power of Christian tradition. This book is an effort to put together theological expertise with the rich spiritual experiences that quietly inform the homes, factories, and offices of laity.

So let this broad audience be warmly welcomed—and warned. This book will skirt the edges of being "hard going." But so it should be, remembering Jesus' insistence that the love of God must involve "all your mind" (Luke 10:27). If you bog down in certain sections that appear abstract, persevere. Right over the hill will be practical exercises that involve familiar things you can smell and touch.

Another warning is appropriate as well, though it contrasts with the first one. After each exploration of theory, praxis will be forthcoming. We theologians get annoyed sometimes when the application of "what" to "how" and "where" involves mundane experiences and workaday behavior. Yet, in our overreaction to spirituality as sentimentality, we need to take seriously the other part of Jesus' admonition. Love of God "with all your mind" needs to be done "with all your heart, and with all your soul, and with all your strength" (Luke 10:27). Perhaps there is some foundation to the warning that prospective students are sometimes given by laity against the seminary's tendency to rob them of their religion. So a certain humility is in order. There are illiterate third-world peasants with homemade rosaries who know far more profoundly than I the God whom I have been seeking with all my cherished degrees.

With the front of the product now bearing multicolored labels of invitation and caution, let me describe the intended user:

- This book is for those who are troubled with the little they do know about the nature of God and of themselves, who know best what they do not really understand, and who have a hunch that what is most important is that which strikes with the power of a hint. It is not intended for those who are clear about who God is, and about themselves.
- This book is for those of us who, while flooded with experiences of all kinds, do not know how to distinguish the sacred from the secular. Rather, it is for those of us who seem destined to be wooed by the uncommonness of common-day things, and thus for whom belief must remain a disguised hope. It is not intended for those who know what spirituality is, or have experienced rare and undoubtable experiences of the Divine.
- This book is for those of us who look straight at life and "want it all," while knowing that we can never be satisfied, and suspecting that God cannot be either. It is not intended for those who have mastered one dimension of spirituality and are satisfied.
- Finally, this book is for those of us who may have been burned by "churchy things" like prayer and worship, and thus have difficulty being "neutral" even about the word spirituality. Yet we cannot quiet the moments of strange urgency whose depths have the feel of all or nothing.

Part I

Christian Spirituality:
What Is It, and Why?

1

Restlessness as Ache:
Quiet Evening Reflections

Late evening hours can be strange. As long as the television is on and the children are up, there is not much time or space for feelings to work their way in around the edges. As long as I keep busy, life seems to hold together fairly well on automatic pilot. The problem comes when I stop, when I've weathered enough responsibilities to deserve time off for good behavior. That's when the feelings sharpen—after the late news, when the cat is out for the night and I am alone at the kitchen table with a cup of coffee I hardly need.

What I experience is not ordinary anxiety. There will always be bills on the first of the month, and weekly squabbles that characterize even the best of marriages. What I am talking about happens even when things seem to be in place—the lawn mowed, the house painted. The stirrings I am referring to are deep inside, much like an ache rooted in restlessness. It is as if there should be something more. No matter what I have or do, life has about it a feeling of "not quite."

When I was younger, life and work were hardly distinguishable, wrapped up in an effort to render this "not yet" into a "very soon." But that approach no longer seems very promising. Instead, the feel has become an uneasiness lest this and all the "soons" are all that there is! Actually this doesn't make sense. Compared with what many other people have, what more could I want? And yet, "more and more" is taking on the feel of "less and less."

I suspect that the ache may go still deeper. There seems to be an absence that has about it the scent of homesickness—for a place I've never been. This is threatening, for such strangeness is starting to undermine what I already have. Its outer edge is taking on the firmness of an ought. This is ironic—that I ought to do something about what I ought to know, but don't. Here at midnight, in the midst of a house with every convenience, it seems as if I am in an empty room whose emptiness insists upon a fullness *of a different kind.*

If what I am experiencing were all negative, then I might try crowding out the feelings by playing first base on the Wednesday night slow-pitch team. But, actually, I'm intrigued. Strange though it sounds, the persistent whispers I hear hint of a *pregnant* absence—that what seems void is not nothingness. Behind the yearning, there is almost a Luring. True enough, the moon casts over the back porch of my life long shadows—as if something "should not be." Yet the mellow moonlight brings moments whose intensity and depth dare me to call them sacred.

Such moments pass. By morning there remains only an uneasy memory—with the substance of dusty footprints.

The Primal Question

I am not the only one to feel this way. Paul Tillich understood:

> In knowing God as the absent God, we know of [God]; we feel [God's] absence as the empty space that is left by something or someone that once belonged to us and has now vanished from our view.[1]

Tillich's use of God language can make some of us uneasy. But we would be fooling ourselves not to admit that our strange talk is pointing to the edges of what for centuries the church has called spirituality.

We may be discouraged from acknowledging this because spokespersons for the recent resurgence of spirituality often seem to discredit the restlessness we are describing. In fact, we could easily gain the impression that for them spirit life tolerates no doubt. There seems to be little room for "maybes," for "what ifs," or even for belief punctuated by "buts." Faith, it would appear, entails the certainty that belongs only to yes or no, true or false, believer or atheist. As a result, for those of us plagued with the absence of something, the language of spirituality can seem alien, even offensive. We are the ones for whom certitude seems destined to be built from hints glued together with hope. But even if others view our efforts as a confederation of Scotch tape and bobby pins, let us at least take pride in the fact that we begin at the point where primal questions fight for clarity. And when we roll our assorted strangeness into a verbal question, it sounds like this: What are we to do with the longing for a "more" that is "beyond," for a "beyond" that is "within," for a "within" that is "all," and for an "all" that insists upon remaining "mystery"?

Resources for a Dilemma No Longer Individual

If that question makes strange sense, you too may be one of the "bitten ones." We are a strange lot, not only in religious circles but in secular ones as well, for the computer world of "binary ex- actitude" also insists that things be programmed into yes or no, for or against. Mystery isn't a conversation piece around the water cooler. To the contrary, computers are symbolic of our dilemma. Even the user-friendly models keep asking, "Are you sure?" And the grouchy models sound downright ominous: "Warning/Error/ Invalid Entry/Press Escape."

Yet "mystery" is really our code word—for "hope." But hope for what? The hope is that this ache for more, translated as a pri- mal question, *is more than an omen of personal failure.* I need to believe that this nibbling inside me is an indictment, as well, of modern life—a question mark tunneled into the daily ads of our self-indulgence.

In my first efforts to force-feed this hope into some sort of spir- ituality, the piety of my past kept intruding. For many of us, it isn't that our childhood "spirituality" is merely inadequate. It is an actual roadblock, for we have been burned by it. Even for those who have licked their wounds into scar tissue, often only a glance at the current crop of popular "spiritual" resources brings forth a severe knee-jerk reaction.

It is little wonder, then, that many of us seem pushed to explore resources that are novel. Surely, somewhere, there is an answer. So, if raised a Protestant, one sifts for treasures among the twice-told traditions of Catholicism. Certain Roman Catholics, in turn, are drawn toward the Protestant charismatics for inspiration, while others explore scripture with such fervor that they threaten to become contemporary Luthers.

Meanwhile, as this unofficial Christian exchange program takes on the choreography of a fruit-basket upset, other searchers aban- don Western religion for the hors d'oeuvres of Eastern spiritual- ity. Yet those who visit the East often return in dismay. Countries long celebrated for their spiritual foundations are being seduced by Western materialism into buying and selling the parceled earth once called "mother."

As we gaze over this trampled landscape, there is a haunting uneasiness that these spiritual traditions have become too frayed to feed even their own. Shall we start over again? Doing so is easy, Voltaire once mused. "It takes only getting killed, and rising the third day." With that sobering thought, the question returns full circle. Can it be that the interactive searching evident today is signal not that the rich heritage of Christianity is impotent, but that its modern expressions have neglectfully squandered that heritage in rendering it competitive rather than inclusive?

Definition and the Case for Pluralism

The Judeo-Christian tradition into which many of us have been born is, in fact, a tradition amazingly rich and organic. So where does one turn for an introduction? The church, certainly. But here the perplexity becomes embarrassing. We can welcome the fact that spirituality is presently applying for official status at many mainline denominational headquarters. Yet a one-liner capable of embarrassing most Protestant ministers is this: "Pastor, tell me about your spirit life."

The silence is revealing. It conveys not only a dearth of clear practice, and probably even of restlessness, but reflects a confusion about even the subject. What is spirituality? While we are disappointed by such a response or lack thereof, our own mumblings about aches and yearnings hardly qualify as a definition. The dilemma is mutual, then, but none the less alarming, for there is hardly any question more foundational for the church.

Thus, whatever additions we might care to risk later, minimally, *spirituality means living one's theology; theologizing, in turn, means articulating into self-consciousness one's spirituality*. Let's try again. Spirituality is the manner in which a person is oriented in being, through which one's meaning is recognized, embraced, disciplined, and enhanced. Expressed more simply, spirituality is the way in which the whole of me responds to the whole of life. John Macquarrie's definition is even more skeletal: "Spirituality is . . . the process of becoming a person in the fullest sense."[2] Even Calvin insisted that "without knowledge of self, there is no knowledge of God."[3]

Publishers are beginning to sense that spirituality so understood is essential to living—and thus in need of serious resourcing. As a result, there are appearing new diggings into diverse traditions within Christianity, many of which have become encrusted by neglect or misuse. Yet even in such responsible resurrections of denominational heritages, there is still the tendency for them to resemble mutually exclusive alternatives. Thus it could become as true now as it has been in the past that "spirituality was often a factor causing organizational disunity among Protestants." Ironic though it may sound, spirituality has been a central cause in the church's seedy divisiveness. Thus while it is true that "each Protestant tradition may be viewed as a 'school of spirituality,'" the crucial question is this: Will such resurgence resurrect a competitive and fateful denominationalism, or are we at a moment in history that could become a gateway into a new spiritual ecumenism?[4]

Within Roman Catholicism there appears a similar phenomenon, in this case all under the same umbrella. Paralleling Protestant denominationalism, multiple spiritualities have become distilled into distinctive "schools of spirituality" characterizing contrasting religious orders. Thus Ignatian (Jesuit) activism is juxtaposed with Trappist silence, while ascetic Carthusian isolation jars with the Benedictine richness of sung liturgy.

Therefore, instead of establishing a crucible from which a rich, composite spirituality for our times might emerge, the spiritual renewal in both Protestant and Roman Catholic traditions could lead instead to refurbishing the headquarters of rival camps. Even when efforts are made to overcome such exclusivism through some kind of unified spiritual pluralism, the tendency is hardly more promising, for it tends to be done hierarchically. What happens is that one particular approach is identified as the "meat," with other spiritual possibilities reduced to the "milk" of preparation (see Heb. 5:11–14).

Thus what is needed—and this book is an attempt at this—is a rediscovery of the rich beauty of Christian spiritual pluralism, *understood noncompetitively as a whole and made available through concrete practices to become a custom-fitted coat of many colors*. With our assignment finally named and in place, one uneasiness may remain. When restlessness encourages a person to tackle some of the acknowledged spiritual classics, the impression can come quickly that real spirituality is for the intellectually sophisticated—or, even more, for those "called" to be full-time "professional" Christians. The truth is that many saints *were* monks, priests, missionaries, bishops, and theologians, for whom religion was their lifework. Unfortunately, then, one might be tempted to see all others, at best, as spiritual amateurs, condemned to the penance of hearing weekly sermons, mumbling morning prayers at a mirror through shaving cream, and quieting the kids long enough for a blessing over cardboard breakfast food.

It is more than time to develop another approach. What we need is a spirituality that (1) does not require choosing between major spiritual positions, but provides viable pluralistic options that are not alternatives but, rather, invitations to participate in a holistic spirituality; and (2) employs analogies from common-day life through which to identify and name, as already richly present, those potential experiences traditionally called "life in the Spirit."

The God Question and the Functional Gods

The first step toward satisfying this need comes in facing squarely the central question. While Tillich used God language in describing our ache, it appears for some of us to be a huge jump from a "yearning" to a spirituality rooted in a supernatural Someone. In fact, before any yes-or-no decision can be made on the God issue, there is a prior question: What is even meant by the word God?

This whole conversation began, as you recall, with late-night coffee at the kitchen table. You might remember, as well, that in talking of "ache" we came to the conclusion that this was not a yearning for more of the same. The "more" needed to be of a different order. Well, this "more" has a name. In the trade, it is called "God."

A second step follows. "God" is not a proper name, any more than aspirin means Bayer, or "man" is my surname. "God" is a generic term, to be used functionally. God is the basis on which I assume that it is better to live than to die. The choices are many — job, family, country, causes, success, each competing to function as one's "God." The spiritual task becomes serious when restlessness agitates a person to identify with proper name that God which in fact is already functioning as one's lived meaning — probably without one knowing it.

While such an approach may sound strange initially, the results are significant. It means that no one can avoid the God question, for we have no other option than to be plagued by the "why" question, repeatedly. Why death, why life, why bother? Why do I get up in the morning and brave daily the interstate traffic, especially when there are countless things I would rather do? Why do I live in this particular neighborhood, or this very house? Why marriage, or singleness — or why not? Why this job? *Why anything?*

And grounding every such question is the primal question at its base: Why life itself, when death is within my power to choose—socially, psychologically, and physically?

With such questioning, the yearning to which we have referred throughout can become illuminated in a new way: not as the search for a God, but as a deficit balance report concerning the God around which the meaning of one's life is already functioning. Instead of the word God, Tillich preferred the functional phrase "Ultimate Concern." And the truth of one's Ultimate Concern is the degree to which it can be trusted without betrayal and obeyed without idolatry. In a word, the truth of one's God is its *livability*—in depth and breadth. Put as a question, does faith in one's concrete God bring the satisfaction that makes living worthwhile—for one who clearly knows that you go around only once? So put, it becomes apparent how the God question inevitably intersects with the death question. One can become theologically awakened by the thought of closing the cover on a life dedicated only to selling radiator caps. For me, such awakening occurred on my fiftieth birthday, with five words: "It isn't all possible anymore."

While Calvin's God language pointed toward a depraved human nature, our language points more toward a deprived one. Somehow life by the year, stretched out as a hammock between the Super Bowl and the World Series, can take on the feeling of existing without ever having lived.

Spirituality, then, is a universal phenomenon, although it is most often unconscious. Rendering it conscious begins with naming one's functional God. This need becomes urgent when, fumbling at the box of life, one suddenly notices the flap marked "Open Other End." And what is learned in searching for the identity of the God at the center of one's daily "why"? That the process needs to be an undercover operation. One's God often turns out to be largely unknown, unrecognized, and part of our unconscious. Therefore, to name the Name, one must catch oneself in disclosing situations. My God has something to do with when I get threatened, with my favorite chair, the advertisements that appeal to me, my favorite TV shows, my hobbies. By our fruits shall we be known—from the color of my car to the contents of my trunk. What I do reflects who I am; and who I am is reflected in everything I do. I am my record collection, and my books are a down payment on my pilgrimage. My home is a contour map of my soul. The God question, then, is not an issue of if or when, but of what or whom. Israel recognized the functional presence of

many Gods. That is why the people kept asking of the faithfulness
they experienced, "What is [your] name?" (see Ex. 3:13–14).

Now if every person has a God, of necessity the church's spiritual task begins in arranging for each person's Divine-human introduction to take place. "It's about time you two meet." Such a
greeting can bring joyous homecoming for some—as naming the
Name of the One with whom faithfulness brings living, both in
depth and breadth. Such revealing can bring a conscious call to
full and disciplined commitment. For other persons, however,
such an introduction can be a painful encounter, disclosing one's
allegiance as a betrayal of one's real self.

The church, however, is not doing well at providing such intro-
ductions. On the one hand, it has largely failed to recognize this
God question as a task arising from a functional understanding of
God. On the other, it has lost through reduction the richness of
the particular God it has been called to name. Thus it has lost
identity with the universality of the question, and is losing the
ability to name as friend the Shadow behind the question as ache.

How tragic, for, as Evelyn Underhill insisted, God is the interesting thing about religion.

The Pluralistic Self and the Pluralistic God

The momentum of this chapter is bringing us face to face with
the two key dilemmas on which the remainder of this book will
rest. Ironically, in considering them together, a fascinating solution emerges: *The ability to establish a viable pluralistic spirituality emerges hand in hand with a rediscovery of the Christian
God as pluralistic.* The clue for which many of us seek, unknowingly, is provided for by one of the strangest, least understood,
and most neglected of Christian doctrines: the Trinity.

Whatever subtleties there might be around its edges, Trinity is
the insistence that *God is richly pluralistic, within and without.*
To say this in a related way, the Sacred is thoroughly relational,
both by nature and by choice. What follows is that spirit life, by its
very nature, is composed of pluralistic experiences and relationships. An analogy may be helpful. Close friendship is hardly possible between two persons who have only one kind of relation. To
know one of my colleagues only as colleague is to have, at best, a
working acquaintance. To become a deep friend, by contrast, I
need to know him as a laughing confidant over thick-crust pizza, a
first-base side Royals fan, an angry poet, a fellow dreamer, one
who aches at the piano after midnight—and one inclined to open

life's flaps at the wrong end. So with the Christian God. To know God only as the dark at the top of the stars is not to have a friend.

Spirituality is the total relation of the whole person to the Whole of life. For the Christian, then, mutual friendship with this Whole in whose image we have been created must, of necessity, be richly pluralistic. The church's gift of the Trinity brings bad news and it brings good news. The bad centers, as we have suggested, in recognizing that the disquieting ache at the kitchen table is not simply for some God in general. The absence is evidence that one's God is too small, incapable of bearing rich friendship. It is a hunger for One with whom we can have multiple relations. The good news, on the other hand, is that the absence is in truth a hunger, pulling heavily upon our imagination, stretching it into dissatisfaction with any vision less than seeing and hearing Presence almost everywhere. Augustine's classic words stand as fine recognition of this correlation between our pluralistic yearning and the nature of the God in whose triune image we have been created: "O Lord, thou hast made us for thyself, and restless is our heart until it comes to rest in thee."[5]

Redeeming Secular Experience

With this correlation named, how can we come to experience such plural relationships? Here the depth of the spiritual crisis in our time becomes most apparent. Common-day experiences have become so secularized that we seem to have passed a threshold beyond which there is no turning back—into a desacralized world no longer fit as an arena for forging spirit. Just to raise the issue of spirituality in our time is to risk becoming prodigal. A glance at advertisements in *Newsweek* or an evening spent sampling the local movie fare are sufficient to recognize that this is no longer the old cosmic neighborhood that religious folk once called home. We feel that we are living in the far country, not because we have left home, but because home has left us. Some of us are tempted by warm memories to sit on the fence of the old homestead as old beliefs and practices not vacated by night are auctioned off cheaply. And, as we watch, it is hard to imagine anymore what a spiritual experience might be like.

One can hardly overstate the significance of a Sputnik sweeping clean the space we once called the heavens. Or the import of making dirty footprints on a moon whose mystery once enthralled both mystic and lover. Or the meaning of strewing our mechanical trash among the stars. In the backwash of scientific utility, is there anything left in the spiritual trunks — stuff we could try on at least for fun, like children in the attic on a rainy Sunday afternoon? For some, all that remains are faint remembrances of Bible stories, painted with that sentimental aura characteristic of the improbable. And even if scripture could be resurrected as spiritual guide, would it not push us toward a dualism smacking of schizophrenia? We seem to have reached a point of no return in history, where from now on any spirituality considered viable must resist the rupture between secular and sacred, the sealing of inner from outer, the alienating of physical from spiritual, and the estranging of our "doing" from our "being."

This loss centers in the difficulty of identifying *in common-day experience* any dimensions begging to be baptized as spiritual. We are tempted to abandon the "spiritual" to someone else, who is somewhere else, doing something else. Yet there may be another possibility open to those of us who want to believe that experiences once called spiritual might still be possible, somehow. At the far end of that hope appears a hunch — that the problem is not one of absence, but rather that in this twilight time of our modernity such experiences can only strike us *with the power of hints*.

If so, what is needed are new images and metaphors evocative enough to tease into speech the guesses called forth by such hints. The recovery of spirituality in our day, then, would have little to do with gaining new experiences. We are already drowning in an overload of sensations. The recovery will entail a deepening of the ones we already have, by naming as spiritual the tender nuances of common-day experience capable of making life richly worthwhile. This effort will require the construction of exercises out of analogies sufficiently familiar to render visible the "invisibility" which was once readily known as spirit life.

What stands before us is a twofold task. First, the Christian God needs to be understood in a way that provides a theological foundation for spiritual experiences as pluralistic. Second, we must so focus daily experiences that through discipline they may become apertures through which the meaning of God becomes a holistic spiritual life-style.

Gift Through Contradiction

We end these beginning thoughts with a caution. Some theologians insist that spirit life is a gift, for which the only valid preparation is a confession of spiritual poverty. There is truth in this

affirmation; otherwise the Christian God becomes an advertise-
ment for self-help. Yet a second affirmation is equally true, embracing the first in a savory paradox. Spirituality as gift occurs
most readily in the midst of contradiction.

An autobiographical illustration might help. Spirituality as gift
came powerfully when I was forced by the dead-end ache of serving the Protestant work ethic as God into the terrifying silence of a
Trappist monastery. There, in the paradox of strange opposites, a
Protestant mind and a Catholic heart gently made love—and gave
rebirth to each other. Because neither "doing" nor "being" could
have its way alone, the resolution was the gift spelled grace. Several years later, my pilgrimage again led into the powerful valley
of paradox. This time, a gregarious, extroverted "me" entered my
"shadow" side—living a life of solitary introversion as a hermit for
six months. Ironically, this heavy trek into the desert experience
gifted me with a light and childlike joy simply in being alive.

For most of us today, it is likely that viable spirituality will entail placing ourselves in those places where gift is most likely to be
born through contradiction. This may mean having one's Protestant wordiness quieted by forced listening—until plaintive winds
through solitary pines give birth to the Quaker roots within. Activists may need the dark morning hours, where the mystic's
claim to "soul sickness" as a sacred gift can break through the web
of Messianic doing. For still others, the cure might be a forced
lyricism, puncturing the balloon of pompous self-importance by
replacing one's suit and tie with a Mickey Mouse T-shirt. And for
those whose prayer life is a patronizing folksiness with a benevolent grandfather, the hope for gift may arise within the stench of
third-world poverty.

Ironically, it is because spirituality *is* a gift that our responsibility for it must be intensified—to be where a branding by contradiction is most likely to occur. Such a place is likely to be where
one is forced to look back on a life that one may be on the verge of
losing by not living. Henri Nouwen understands.

> The paradox of prayer is that we have to learn how to pray, which
> we can only receive as a gift. . . . We cannot plan, organize, or ma-
> nipulate God; but without a careful discipline, we cannot receive
> [God] either.[6]

Naming the Name

Such contradictions come with assorted sizes and shapes of
faces and names. I share one of mine as a blessing for this journey

that we are taking together. This particular face peeked out of a nun's habit, answerable to the name Sister Dominique. Having come to a dead end in my search for some special experience that could be called spiritual, I was directed to this "God-intoxicated woman." I disliked her immediately. She oozed spirituality. She knew too much. Even so, that was no excuse for my heavy touch of cynicism.

"Is it too much to ask for one clear experience of God? After all, Saint Teresa of Avila had emotional orgies with God for years." I felt better.

"Have you ever known any kind of ecstasy?" she wryly probed.

"Sure." With a slight recklessness, I described my experiences with music.

Her laughter cut my babbling short. I was hurt.

"Do you realize what you just said?" Obviously not. I waited, poised with ready defensiveness.

"Your description of being lost in music sounds precisely like Teresa's description of her ecstasy with the Divine. *Who robbed you of the ability to name the Name?*"

She would not stop.

"What do you do for Vespers?" She was getting embarrassing.

"Not much," I ventured.

"Well, then, what do you do when you come home from work?"

"I check in with folks, share a glass of wine, try to let go, and listen to music."

"What music?"

"Well, some days it's Telemann; others, Mozart; or maybe the blues—you know, whatever the Spirit . . . " I faltered.

Again came the laughter. I was caught.

"Paul, who has robbed you even of the words? Your ending of the day could well serve as outline for the way the church has celebrated Vespers for ages. Pick up your bed and walk." To name the Name into recognition.

T. S. Eliot knew what she meant, although it has taken me years to be sure. He spoke of having the experience but "missing the meaning."[7] Missing the meaning. That is what this book is about.

2

The Trinity:
Can Even the Idea
Make Sense Anymore?

We have reason to conclude that the array of opinions, experiences, and approaches collectively called "spirituality" can be so confusing that one scarcely knows where to begin. Consequently, we searchers often find ourselves on a pilgrimage with no clear direction, toward a goal equally vague, pushed on by an unsettling absence. And the serious sources that are available can appear to be so complex, so varied, and so "learned" that one may be discouraged from trying. Furthermore, the methods developed by these celebrated champions of the spirit life can appear to be mutually exclusive, or at least highly competitive. Thus our converging dilemma. If a person must choose one particular spiritual stance in order to experience the "spiritual," how can those of us without conscious spiritual experience know which one to choose?

Such confusion has been pushing us toward a spirituality which by its nature is pluralistic. This involves abandoning two popular efforts: to synthesize spirituality into a least common denominator, and/or to arrange spirit options in a hierarchical arrangement of ascending importance. In contrast, our approach will attempt to make contact with the present pluralistic age, at the same time rendering meaningful the Christian understanding of a triune God.

Pluralism and Art

Making sense out of the idea of pluralistic spirituality can be helped by an analogy from art history. No major school of painting can be declared better than all the others. Some painters are pioneers, while others distill well the genius of a particular type—and each of us has favorites. But none of the fine arts can be understood as evolutionary movements toward a purer and eventually ultimate aesthetic achievement. On the contrary, the history of each art form, by its very nature, is pluralistic; and the rich meaning of each form belongs to the ongoing whole. That whole is never to be emptied out or finally captured by any of its parts. Thus it makes no sense to insist that Frank Lloyd Wright's Guggenheim Museum is superior to the Great Pyramid. Nor can one declare that Cézanne's work captures better than Van Gogh's the meaning of painting, or that Beethoven was "right" and Mozart was "wrong." Nor can drama be understood as footnotes to Shakespeare's plays. Nor can the person who loves music ever be satisfied playing only one type of music, or pieces from one period. Love of music is rooted in a passion for the rich and inexhaustible nature of sound as such, just as the possibilities of drama are infinite for those intoxicated by the smell of greasepaint.

To appreciate only études, or sonnets, or landscapes is neither to know nor to love music, poetry, or painting. So it is with spirit life. While it is helpful to distinguish spirit types, this dare not be done for the purpose of hierarchical evaluation or for justifying exclusivity. The rich variety is itself the seamless garment in which the meaning of spirituality is clothed. And immersion in its profound contrasts is what gives fiber to the whole. Insatiability and intoxication are the telltale signs of the lover.

The Dual Approaches to God

To insist upon spirituality as pluralistic is to be pushed straight into the God question. And at the heart of Christianity is the insistence that God too is pluralistic. Trinity is the declaration that God relates to creation and to persons in multiple ways, never to be emptied out—any more than Wagner marked the end of opera, or Dante rendered consequent efforts in poetry a tiresome paraphrase.

The Trinity has been an ongoing way of distilling a great deal of wisdom about God gained over the centuries. The two basic understandings of Trinity that have resulted really arise from the two fundamental ways in which God tends to be experienced. The first is the Positive Way ("cataphatic"). It emerges as a gasp in seeing a V of geese flying south in the vesper sun. It has something to do with the first snowfall, when no footprints mar the innocence.

One feels it when a gentle rain paints a spring meadow with special green, or the wind fingers the golden tassels at harvesttime. These are the moments of "too much" aching for the "more" of another intensity. And, if one lets them float toward their yearning level, they are raised to the infinite power. Expressions of life all around us, at least for the moment, become attributes that point—light, goodness, love, birth—"linking sense to sound and sight." And where in the imagination they converge, that is what is meant by God.

The church has long rummaged among such experiences for some of its favorite God names: Infinite Light, All Glorious Creator, O Perfect Love, Majestic Mystery, "pavilioned in splendor." Music often says it best:

> Not angel tongues can tell thy love's ecstatic height,
> the glorious joy unspeakable, the beatific sight.
> > "Maker in Whom We Live"[1]

In the words of another hymnist,

Word of God from nature bringing
Springtime green and autumn gold;
Mountain streams like children singing,
Ocean waves like thunder bold:
Alleluia, Alleluia, as creation's tale is told.
> "God, Whose Love is Reigning O'er Us"[2]

In this approach, God becomes the name for the inexhaustibility of a child's smile, coupled with a confession of our utter inability to grasp the "magic" of a spring morning. All such things point to, because they participate in, a perfect Beauty, an ultimate Mystery. This is the "more" of another Intensity, in which everything is grounded, and for which everything aches.

The second approach for experiencing God is the Negative Way ("apophatic"). It is in times of weariness that I touch this way best—when living resembles carousel horses that go up and down, barely getting back to the point from which they began. These are the times when it would be enough for me to be able to stand in the unmoving center of the whole thing and be quiet. There I could be one with the still point of the turning wheel, yearning for that which is complete in "itself," needing nothing else in order to be.

In the first approach, that which attracts is God as immanent, as if we are being lured by One who is in and with and by and for every particle that is. In the second, we stand as the infinitely small before the Infinitely Transcendent, quieted by a longing for

that which is utterly different in kind—as Pure, Holy, Infinite,
Eternal, or as the hymnist Walter Chalmers Smith said it, "un-
resting, unhasting, and silent as light."

> Immortal, invisible, God only Wise,
> in light inaccessible hid from our eyes, . . .
> we blossom and flourish as leaves on the tree,
> and wither and perish, but naught changeth thee.
>   "Immortal, Invisible, God Only Wise"[3]

Most of us are touched by something of this experience in
watching the yearly rerun of *The Wizard of Oz*. It threatens to
become "too much" when Judy Garland sings about birds flying
over the rainbow, and pleads, "Why, then O why, can't I?" How
shall we interpret the tears? It seems to do with what we are not,
and therefore God "has" to be. Eyes go instinctively closed, shut-
ting out the outside world as one goes deeply inside, into the craving and beyond the dreaming. The mystics lead the way, knowing
beyond knowing that such efforts to know God internally strain
the intellect, until in emptiness it breaks open into Silence—in an
intuitive "cloud of unknowing."[4] One enters the Abyss, as it
were, and becomes the Mystery. In the "dark night of the soul,"
the senses are unable to satiate the longing. Yet, ironically, it is
this same darkness which can expose an Otherness in absence,
rending our nothingness into a recognition that the very fact of
our existing is gift—hand-wrapped in a shroud.

We can characterize these two approaches to the God experience as that of the "awe" and that of the "ache." Unfortunately,
these are often treated as if they were mutually exclusive. The result is a dualism of immanence versus transcendence, doing versus being, worldly versus otherworldly. Yet, for some of us, the
spiritual meaning that is beginning to emerge seems to be slung
between the necessity for both such moments. In the first type of
experience, one's wide-eyed face is brushed with an intensity that
could want nothing more. In the second, often in darkness, the
longing knows that there is nothing in this life that can ever fully
satisfy. The first kind of experience is mediated through what *is*;
the second is mediated through what *is not*. And somehow they
are woven together, much as front is to back, purgation is to illumination, less is to more. On the one hand, the deeper the experience, the deeper the hunger. On the other, the more insatiable
the longing, the more it is rooted in what has already been experienced as foretaste.

Even mystics as varied as Teresa of Avila, Julian of Norwich, and Jakob Böhme experience both approaches — interweaving absence with presence, negative with positive, ascetic with sensual, otherworldly with earthy, and eternal with temporal. Böhme expresses the interplay: "In that Light the one sees the other, feels the other, smells the other, tastes the other, and hears the other, and is as if the whole Deity rose up therein."[5]

Thus, while these two basic approaches have sometimes been seen as incongruous, they actually move toward each other in our kitchen experience at midnight — as an absence yearning for presence, and a presence lined with insatiability. Spirituality, then, is an invitation into a dynamic that is both plunging and sweeping, as fully purgative as it is sacramental and rhapsodic.

What follows from such ruminations should come as no surprise. *Our relation to God is likewise pluralistic — or not at all.*

The Christian Triune Encounter — as Manifestation

One could expect, then, that these two ways of experiencing God should impact deeply the way in which the Christian church came to understand the nature and activity of its God. While it took three centuries for the doctrine of the Trinity to be affirmed, it was really an official recognition that God, as pluralistic mystery, is known in the two ways we have been describing. Thus *how* God is pluralistically experienced and *who* God is must be explored together.

Now put this insight on the shelf for a moment, while we explore a second point. The God knowable in these two ways is encountered by the Christian in a unique way — in the event called Jesus Christ. Thus the church insisted that this event provides the clue for understanding how the plural experiences *with* God relate to the plural nature *of* God. The apostle Paul distilled that revelation perceptively: "For it is the God who said, 'Let light shine out of darkness' [God as Creator], who has shone in our hearts [God as Sanctifier] to give the light of the knowledge of the glory of God in the face of Christ" [God as Redeemer] (2 Cor. 4:6). Here Paul's tripartite experience was recognized as revealing a God whose functioning with us is itself triune.

Over the next several centuries, the church explored deeply this insight that an encounter with *how* God acts provides clues as to *who* God is. The conclusion was that any of God's roles, taken in isolation, is insufficient, if not misleading. If one affirms God only as Creator, the fact of evil and tragedy all around us becomes an indictment of such a God. Thus one needs to speak as well of God as Redeemer, the One deeply immersed in rectifying the condition of the world. Yet if the Redeemer is not also the Creator, then we have two Gods locked in a deadly dualism. But even to affirm both of these roles is insufficient. The struggle of the Creator as Redeemer is not liberating if that involvement remains general and impersonal. It needs to be personal, immediate, and deeply intimate, at soul depth. This requires the affirmation that the Creator-Redeemer is Spirit. But if God were only Spirit, God's personal involvement would give only individual solace, providing inner escape from a cosmos and history that remain divinely untouched. The Sanctifying God thus needs to be involved in bringing the whole cosmos to completion. Hereby is God disclosed as Creator-Redeemer-Sanctifier.

Thus our varied experiences of God are seen by the Christian as rooted in a God with multiple roles. Just as my friend is companion, musician, and Royals fan, so the sweeping functions of the One God are triune: as Creator, Redeemer, and Sanctifier—distinguishable, but interrelated. Such an analogy helps clarify why the church used terminology that today we find confusing—the part about three "Persons." "Person" had nothing to do with the modern word "personality." If it did, Trinity would mean three Gods, or Divine schizophrenia. Instead, early theologians drew upon an analogy from drama. The "dramatis personae" appearing on the program of a play is a list of roles, with the names of the persons playing them. In early times, an actor would often wear a mask appropriate to the part, making it quite normal for an actor to play multiple "personae" or roles. So God.

We are ready now to relate how this functional description of the triune God makes contact with the Positive and Negative approaches to religious experience with which we began this chapter. The Positive perspective, as we recall, finds powerful analogies in the external world for disclosing the God who participates in and with the world. The traditional name for the understanding of God that results is the Trinity of Manifestation—the God manifested throughout the cosmos. This, then, is the first of the two approaches that the church has used in exploring the meaning of God as triune. It is an external approach, concerned to understand the pluralistic nature of God *in relationship to the cosmos,* in the roles of Creator, Redeemer, and Sanctifier. The second approach, to which we now turn, is internal—*a concern for God as God is in God's own self.*

The Christian Triune Encounter—as Essence

The Negative approach to experiencing God makes use of internal analogies. Here the concern is not to relate to God in terms of God's functionings with the world. Instead, the yearning is to become immersed in God—to lose one's self in the triune God in whom one lives and moves and has one's being.

An illustration may be helpful. Knowing another person entails more than recognizing how she "manifests" herself in various roles. Such activities might fascinate me. But falling in love is to know somehow the person behind all that she "does"—the being behind the doing, as it were. So with God. In the sexual relation there can be moments of this kind, of being lost in each other. But particularly impressive is the quality of relationship that can be forged by a couple growing old together, coming so to participate in each other's lives that they can speak and feel for each other. There are intimate evenings by the fireside, when, without a word, communication is near complete. So with God.

My spiritual director is a mystic who rises at 1:30 A.M. "What do you do?" "Nothing." "Then why do you get up at 1:30 A.M.?" "To be in the Presence." "What do you really want out of life?" His response came quickly, with ease: "To grow old loving my God." With the analogy of fireside evoked, one can understand what it means for him to become lost in God. In a peace beyond understanding, one would want nothing, need nothing, and lack nothing, wrapped complete and whole in a relationship for its own sake. Thus even when spirit life is most personal, it is never private.

To summarize, the first approach often suggests organic analogies, in which God relates to the world much as mind does to body, or part does to whole, or cause does to effect, or ground does to participant.[6] There is a mutuality, in which the cosmos is the breakthrough of God into pilgrimage. The second tends toward the mature self as analogy. An adult put in solitary confinement can remain fully self-conscious without a world, as it were. So it is, insists the church, for God. The triune God is *internally* rich, fully and self-consciously whole, free from any need of any cosmos in order to be. The "good news," then, comes as surprise: the God who has no need of us has willed not to be God without us. The cosmos as God's gift, for its own sake, is the heart of what the church means by grace.

For God, then, to be self-conscious means good news *for us*.

But what does it mean *for God?* Scripture insists that we are cre-
ated in the "image" of this God. Thus our self-consciousness can
be seen as a disclosure of God's own inner life. For us, this in-
volves an "I" and a "me," in incessant dialogical relationship.
Likewise for God. Self-consciousness involves the Divine "I"
("Father") being conscious of selfhood through a "me" as alter ego
("Son") in terms of their dialogical relationship of love ("Spirit").
(For discussion of gender references, see "A Diagram of Spirit
Types," below.)

Augustine probed deeply this idea of the image of God in us,
seeking further analogies for understanding God. One of his most
promising is the functioning of mind. While the mind is a unity, it
operates through the distinguishable functions of will, imagination, and memory. In like manner, God is *internally* triune. The
Trinity of Essence is the name given to this understanding of God
as internally and self-consciously rich—God as God is within
God's self. Implications for spirit life follow directly from this second understanding of Trinity, as they did from the first. Distilled
in a sentence, to experience one's selfhood in depth is to experience participation in the inner life of God. Full self-consciousness
means the immersion of one's self as trinity into Trinity, and the
reverse.

The Trinity of Manifestation, then, is an expression of the Positive approach to God, experiencing the diverse dimensions resulting from God's pluralistic relationship with the world. The
Trinity of Essence, on the other hand, is an expression of the Negative approach. Here, through the rich pluralism of one's own
self, is a unifying participation in the diverse unity of God's own
Self, where to become lost is to find oneself in Being itself.

Putting All This Together

Where does such apparently abstract Christian thinking leave
us? With a genuinely pluralistic God as the basis for a richly inclusive spiritual life. The question now is how to envisage these two
understandings of Trinity so that they do not become competitive, providing instead the basis for this spirituality of creative interaction. Hilary of Poitiers provided, in the fourth century, an
exciting idea for doing this, even though it was never fully explored.[7] He insisted that we cannot do justice to the richness of
God and thus to ourselves if we reduce God as "Father" to the
function of Creator, the "Son" to that of Redeemer, and the
"Spirit" to that of Sanctifier. All of God, he insisted, is involved in

every function, not part of God in each. Thus God the Father functions uniquely as creator, redeemer, and sanctifier; likewise, the Son functions in unique ways as creator, redeemer, and sanctifier; and so, in turn, does the Spirit.

Here is an exciting clue for resolving the present spiritual dilemma. *The interaction of God's internal nature and God's external functioning provides a theological basis for exploring as diverse practice the richly varied nature of Christian spirituality.*[8] We can sense psychologically some beginning implications. For extroverts, the Trinity is most easily grasped as "manifest"— perceiving God's self-portrait as cosmos. Yet this is the same God more available for introverts "essentially"—as interior experience of "the inner presence of the Trinity."[9] These are not two Gods. Nor are these two rival spiritualities. What we have are the "positive" and "negative" approaches to spirituality that we explored earlier, recognized by Christians as the two necessary and interrelated ways of experiencing their triune God. This not only validates the spiritual postures most natural for both extroverts and introverts, but in holding them together as mutually necessary each can behold in the other its own shadow or undeveloped side. Thus strengths call forth weaknesses to pilgrimage together toward a holistic spirituality.

One last dab of theory completes our theological grounding. We have related God's internal richness by analogy to the nature of the self. Thus God as triune also means that God by nature is interpersonal. That is, the world created in God's image is by nature a social one. Consequently, the richly relational nature of God is both ground and foretaste of God's organic vision for the cosmos. God by nature and all things by hope are destined for interrelated completeness in the God who is becoming All-in-All. Thus Trinity is an expression of solitariness and community, both for God and for us, as the two poles of a viable, interactive spirituality.

A Diagram of Spirit Types

Our concern in this chapter has been to explore the rich diversity within God and within God's ways of relating to the world. If we consider each Person of the Trinity as being involved in each "function" or "manifestation" of God as Creator, Redeemer, and Sanctifier, we can identify symbolically nine dimensions of God's life, as it were, each inviting our response according to the nature of that dimension. Thus, for example, God as Father/Mother is

MULTIPLE SPIRITUALITY AND THE TRIUNE GOD

TRINITY OF MANIFESTATION

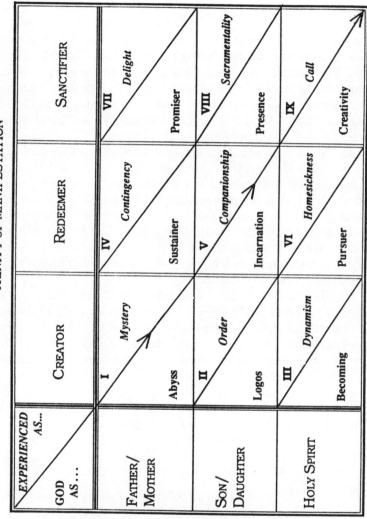

EXPERIENCED AS... GOD AS...	CREATOR	REDEEMER	SANCTIFIER
FATHER/ MOTHER	I *Mystery* Abyss	IV *Contingency* Sustainer	VII *Delight* Promiser
SON/ DAUGHTER	II *Order* Logos	V *Companionship* Incarnation	VIII *Sacramentality* Presence
HOLY SPIRIT	III *Dynamism* Becoming	VI *Homesickness* Pursuer	IX *Call* Creativity

TRINITY OF ESSENCE

Creator, Redeemer, and Sustainer, with these three modes suggesting a way of exploring spirituality as diverse practice in response to the diversity of God's "parenthood."

In our diagram "Multiple Spirituality and the Triune God," the column on the left represents the internal richness of God, and the movement from left to right suggests the Divine functioning in regard to the world. The words on either side of the diagonal drawn through each block suggest the interplay of God's being and God's doing, and thus the way in which one can experience God in relation to the world, contrasted with experiencing God in undifferentiated unity. The left triangles, then, express "dimensions" of God, while the right triangles indicate our experience of them in the world. Each block is numbered for ease of reference as we explore each spirit type in turn.

In developing such a chart, the sexist nature of traditional language arises. Although the motive is well intended, we have recognized the mistake in reducing the "essential Trinity" to the Trinity of Manifestation by identifying "Father" with "Creator," "Son" with "Redeemer," and "Spirit" with "Sanctifier." Thus, to regain the original intent, we will retain the traditional terminology, attempting to neutralize the sexist connotations by providing the opposite gender as well (Father/Mother, Son/Daughter). The biblical word for Spirit is itself feminine. The nine intersections themselves will contribute to the nonsexist richness needed today within theological language.

The chart is also helpful in approaching "heresy." The church's channel markers should indicate that heresy rests not so much in what is said as in what is not said. Thus "liberals" become preoccupied with God as Father/Mother, "orthodox" with God as Son/Daughter, and "charismatics" with God as Holy Spirit. God as creator, in turn, can become too exclusively the domain of "mystics," God as redeemer of the "evangelicals," and God as sanctifier of "activists." "Ortho-praxis" is a name for unity through the practice of pluralism.

A Quick Look Forward

In the chapters that follow, we will work through each of the nine spirit types that correspond to the diversity within God and God's way of relating to the world. Each will be developed in an extended meditation, as an invitation to "feel" as well as "think" one's way into that mode. As invitatory and personal, the hope is so to draw persons into each Christian spirit style that they will want to explore each of them personally. Thus each meditation is followed by a series of expansive and practical spiritual exercises through which each spirit type can be practiced.

We do this with a twofold hope. First, that by discovering intentionally certain aspects of various spirit types, one may discern them as readily available in one's daily context. Second, once recognized, one can render these deeper meanings, through discipline, into a way of life.

A personal illustration may help. I had a terrible time learning to swim. I was a skinny kid, with the buoyancy of a concrete block. While well intended, my mad thrashing simply set records for nasal water consumption. It was all to no avail. The harder I tried, the more my sinking moved in a backward direction. Even to imagine what it would be like to swim was beyond me. Then the day came. Somehow I took three quick strokes—and actually moved! In that moment, for the first time in my life, I had a "feel" for swimming. That was all it took. The threshold was passed. The rest was a matter of practice.

So in spirit life. Most of us have the desire, many of us have the energy, and some of us have the will—but to no avail. Such it has been for me. The problem rests in the absence of any real "feel" for the "what it would be like." As a result, discipline accomplishes little. Teresa of Avila understood this, and gave wise advice in training her novices. The secret, she insisted, rests neither in profound thinking nor in elaborate analysis. It rests in "learning how to look."

The purpose of this book is to learn how to look. It is sufficient if through these nine engagements one might find oneself taking a few first strokes—in alternative ways of looking, and thus of being. One hopes what will follow will be disciplined practice, rendering habitual those exercises which promise to feed. Through each spirit type one sees a piece of the whole. Through each, one sees the whole from one piece. Each is needed, and all—like blowing the trumpet at full moon, rendering everything a feast day (Ps. 81:3).

A Quick Look Backward

Our efforts in this chapter have rested quietly on two premises. Merlin Stone knows the first. Our images of Deity "guide perception, condition us to think and even perceive in a particular way."[10] God is the name for the perspective through which each of us actually sees and hears and touches and smells and tastes life.

Matthew Fox knows the second, coming from the opposite direction: "To alter one's understanding of prayer even slightly is to change the whole course of one's life."[11] The purpose of this book is to join these two premises functionally. If the image of God as triune hones one's eyes to experience life as deeply pluralistic, then the whole course of one's life is changed. And if one's spirit life is changed, the whole course of one's life becomes a relationship with God as "length, breadth, height, depth."[12]

There may be one further premise, hoping to become a conclusion. Our spiritual poverty today may turn out to be not an "absence" after all. We do have experiences which, for those with eyes to see, resemble what was once called spiritual. Simply to have the craving may be the mark of having been found. What we have lost are the meanings, for we no longer know how to name the Name.

Part II

Spiritual Practices:
Multiple Approaches
to a Pluralistic God

3

Getting Lost
in the Silence

Type 1: Mystery

Deep at the center of everything that is, lurking and haunting and nibbling at its edges, is the tendency not to be. Everything rusts, or rots, or breaks, or decomposes, or dies. Nothing remains—at least not for long. Aging makes it personal. We stand daily in front of the bathroom mirror, watching the slow dynamic of less and less. Expressed visually, it is as if the existence of each thing forms a circle, returning to the nothing out of which it came. This cannot be doubted. All that is in doubt is the precise time when the circle will be completed.

Can such relentlessness become part of an orderly pattern, one we can learn to live with? Only for a while. In the deep midnight moments there is a troubled feeling that maybe nothing at all was ever really "meant to be." How shattering, to think that I happened by chance, and you did, and the whole business did. It's hard to face tomorrow's traffic armed with the thought that everything has the stability of a cosmic afterthought. Everyone hurries on the freeways so as not to be late, as if it all makes great sense—soggy jelly-bread sandwiches and all. Yet if death is the destiny with which each of us was stamped somewhere along the birth canal, the fact that anything exists *at all* appears blatantly contradictory.

The Ground of Being

To feel deeply this bottom edge of everything is to be close to where the religious dimension is born. It lurks in the question, Why anything rather than nothing? If nothingness appears to be the "normal" state of affairs, then the fact that anything *does* exist is miracle. The sheer fact of anything and everything thereby becomes inexplicable. This spirit type is born, then, in the awareness that all things, by their very nature, are *radically contingent*. Let's try again. Nothing that exists can account for the fact that it did *come into being*. And nothing that exists can account, in any moment, for the fact that it *continues* to exist.

Truly to see this one fact brings a startling conclusion: that the nonexistence of a Ground of Being for everything is no longer entertainable. Without constant Undergirding, nothing would be. Yet things are. Thus, to experience in truth what it means for anything to exist is to experience in that same moment a "That" which cannot *not* exist, without rendering everything a total self-contradiction. One either sees this or one doesn't. To see it is to experience God as hint within this spirit mode; if one doesn't, then not even the God question makes sense.

An analogy may be helpful. Think of electricity. We flip the switch when we need light, and we have it. This seems so predictable and available that we soon take it for granted. It is always there. Right? Wrong! A transformer blows, plunging the neighborhood into darkness. We wiggle the switch helplessly. Nothing, nothing at all. And there is nothing to be done. The feeling is one of helplessness. In confusion, we ask a stupid question: "Where did the light go?" It didn't go anywhere. It either is or it isn't—and it just isn't! Precisely. *And that is the situation with every single thing that exists.* There will be such a moment—then nothing. Inside one's own self is where this fact seems to live, making strange noises in the quiet hours. Can you feel it? With one wayward skip of the heart, one will not be around, ever, not even to wiggle the switch. This is *the* universal fact. Awareness of its inevitability comes equipped with two words: "Oh, no!" And with them, one knows what we're talking about as the basis of this spirit mode.

The Mystery Inside

But how can this reckoning bring a positive experience, anything that could be called spiritual? The other side of the shock is the awareness of being Grounded. Here one passes over the threshold into *Mystery*. One is touched by it in the awe felt in standing with bare feet in the presence of a fact now rendered sacred—that anything *is*. The issue is not *what* I am, or what I or anything *can* be, or what we or they together *could* do. These questions steer us toward other spirit types. The issue here is *that* I am or anything is. The focus is on Mystery—in and around and at the basis of everything, just because it is. The deeper such hints are sensed, the more one can be overwhelmed, lost as reverent guest in the Silence of the whole. This spirit type centers in the "feel" of the whole of me immersed in the Whole of that which truly is.

Where does one touch such mystery? Above all, one touches it inside. To enter the interior of one's own life is to experience the texture characterizing the inside of life *at any point,* where everything finite is touched into existence by the Undergirding Ground of life itself. Thus this mode of spirituality can be touched everywhere, readily.

But here we encounter an irony. Like electricity, we take life for granted, until it fails. Instead of standing in thankful reverence for every moment, or any moment, we become obsessed by how much of it we can control. Why? Because to admit that we are not really in control of life, *ever,* would "freak us out." It would be like looking down, only to see one's feet resting on nothingness over the abyss of death.

The Mystery Outside

We are inclined, then, to touch this spirit mode first inside ourselves. But it can be touched outside as well, if we know where to look. Remember a crisp fall night, the kind where the Milky Way is slopping all over the picture frame of its horizons. Or perhaps you made a turn in the trail, and there was a doe. What we are talking about occurred in the surprise—of eyes meeting eyes. Or one can recall the inexpressible strangeness in staring down from the edge of a precipice.

Etched into my own memory are very special times of sacred vividness that introduced me to this spirit mode. There was the silent paddling into the dark secrets of the Everglades. There was the feel of working on my knees twenty-two miles from the mouth of a coal mine. There was that special trudging on sand dunes whose shifting marked the unstable edges of the Mojave desert. There was the relentless wind on wheat as it rode the Nebraska prairie toward a sleepy twilight.

Such moments are no more distant than counting the grains in a handful of sand. Wherever it happens, in that moment one is touched by the mystery of anything, hinting of the possibility of immersion into the innate impossibility of everything—and thus the miracle of it all. "To be or not to be"—that is the "enwonder-ment." When such moments sink their teeth into a person, one is on the edge of what mystics are all about: becoming lost in the contemplation of sheer Being.

Expressions East and West

The negative expressions of this mode characterize the spiritu-ality to which Eastern thought points with power. Zen Buddhism attempts to thrust the self directly into the enigma of existing as self-contradiction: I who am becomes I who am not, in order to know without knowledge the unknowableness of Nothingness. Nonsense. Precisely. But it is in confronting variations on such a primal contradiction that one becomes the mystery, negating all separation in reunion. The Western church, on the other hand, favors the positive image of "Abyss" more than that of "Nothing-ness." God as bottomlessness and endlessness is *pregnant,* as it were—for the Abyss in which we are grounded is infinitely cre-ative. The Father/Mother is Creator.

Thus Eastern sensitivity is nurtured by imagery evoking return to the primal womb. Western imagery, on the other hand, focuses on the role of midwife. In the East, the stress is on the diastole—the unity of return of all things to the centered Nothingness, which is All. In the West, the emphasis falls on the systole—the overflowing of being without end.

Experientially, Eastern spirituality, in chanting an "Om" as ex-pressive of this primal nonact, images everything as dissolved into sound, a sound that begins and ends in silence. Understood in a more Western way, the "Om" distills the hum of each motor, the coo of all doves, the whine of every breeze. It is the yearning sound of the pregnant emptiness of the cosmos in the longing sweep of its infinite and enfolding spaces.

Word Silence

Even the most eloquent words falter in describing this spirit type, for words presume a distinction between subject and ob-ject. But it is precisely that separation which this spirit mode de-nies as final. My interior edge and the edge of God are fused—for the Mother/Father God as Creator is the Ground in which all that is lives and moves and has its being. To lose myself in such Noth-ingness is to discover myself in a state of being where I have never known myself to be before, in which nothing more is desired. All separation is overcome in unity.

Acknowledging the inadequacy of any description, still those who have savored this spirit mode use phrases to point: the Primal Source, Infinite Ground, Maternal Mystery, the Nonorigination of Origination, the Becoming of Being, Godhead, Fountainhead, Depth, Center. Visually expressed, the color that encompasses all colors is no color. Since such images can only point, we need them all, whispered in quietness at twilight. Still, when all is said, Meister Eckehart's wisdom pervades: "There is nothing so much like God as silence."

Mystery as Lived

So what would it be like to establish this spirit type as a fulcrum for living? It would involve the self finding itself by losing itself, over and over again. One is born and reborn of nothingness, as sacred possibility. Moment by moment, within life given a day at a time, one would receive thankfully, in humility, each fragment of living—as mystery.

At the heart of this spirit mode, one finds the discipline called "contemplation." As we shall explore in a moment, through it one "is called to plunge into that silence and to lose [oneself] there, unable to utter any word . . . for no word can express the mystery of God [or] the mystery of [us] in the presence of God."[1] As described by another Christian mystic, this mode entails losing "myself in the Origin of all that is, in the Ground of my being, in God. In losing myself, I find my true self at its very Center. I return as it were to the Origin of all origins."[2]

Reborn from Nothingness

So understood, one might think it inevitable that we should all experience freely our lives as rooted in this spirituality, but we don't. The irony of the human condition, as we mentioned, is that we resist this spiritual state. Thus to enter it requires discipline, through a way we have acknowledged as frightening. Simply to become self-conscious in this infinitely vast cosmos is a beginning, for it makes us freaks. To be human is to know, as the billions of living things all around us do not know, that we will die. With this one awareness comes a terrifying loneliness, for none of us belongs any longer.

Sin is the name the church gives to our negative response to the temptation that seems inevitably to follow. To a person, we try to clothe the nakedness of our smallness by squandering the mystery of it all in the arrogant demand to control the uncontrollable. Such reactions provide powerful clues to the erosion of spirituality in our time. We take everything for granted—above all, life itself. Therefore, many of us, instead of accepting the invitation to become reverent guests, live out the abusive presumption of being entrepreneurs. Turning our eyes from the mystery of doorless skies, we compete to enter a dead-end door marked "Chairperson of the Board."

Others of us take life for granted, not through this active bravado of ownership, but through the passive posture of acquiescence. As a boy, I showed everything to my pets. The turtle was hopelessly inattentive, and the goldfish just blinked her mindless eye. But Skippy, my dog friend, had to be different. I remember one night showing him the stars. He wouldn't look. I held his head tight, his nose pointed right at Orion. Nothing. His nose simply wiggled to the scent of something not belonging to the Milky Way. He was so much a part of "the way things were" that awareness was beyond him. So humans can become. I have been lonely ever since.

Whichever box our contamination comes in, to trade it in for a shroud of mystery is about as unlikely as dogs falling in love with stars. And so, while type 1 is a natural beginning for spirituality, it is closed for most of us—unless we become shaken to our roots.

> "Make us know the shortness of our life
> that we may gain wisdom of heart"
> (Ps. 89:12, Paulist [Hebrew, 90:12]).

Such an experience, the "ontic shock" which we will develop in more detail later as central to spirit type 4, is most often evoked by the specter of death. It is only three words away: "You have cancer." In that moment, there is a face-to-face encounter with one's unfathomable finality. This is the finality which most of us spend a lifetime pretending away—while, in truth, it may be our only entrance ticket into spirituality.[3]

Nevertheless, this powerlessness against nothingness is the destiny we share with each thing that exists—but a destiny that only humans can know. And to know it is to be blessed. That is what this first spirit type is about. The positive flip side of this frightful threshold is an awareness that what is true at the moment of my death has been unconsciously true of every moment of my life. Just as I cannot say "No" in the face of death, so the *fact* of every moment of my living is not in my hands either. To be awakened is to behold each instant as a gift, specially wrapped with a personal note.

EXERCISES

Experiencing this spirit type entails nothing more (or less) than perceiving everything in terms of the ontic rootedness we have been describing. Yet over this mode, as over each mode, we will find a myopia of spirit, making it necessary to practice these alternative ways of seeing. Consequently, the following exercises are provided for the sake of discipline. In each case, the hardest part will be to gain an initial taste for the spirit type. After that, it is a matter of practice. Through the exercises that follow, one can taste; through discipline, the taste becomes acquired.

The following procedure is suggested. Read carefully the meditation provided, perhaps several times. Gain a sense of what that particular spirit mode might be like. Then let your imagination suggest, and furnish, a location personally conducive for your experimentation. For maximum impact in each exercise, imagine what you might need to see, or by what sounds you might best be surrounded. Smell and taste have important implications, and what one fondles has unsuspected power. Provide a focus for your senses. Remember that the initial goal is to gain a hint into the elusive experience at the heart of each particular mode.

1. *Contemplation and the Prayer of Centering*

The mystic experience is a gift. But contemplation, which is a discipline, borders on the mystical as its wharf. The goal is simple, the process difficult, and the method elementary. The goal is to bring the mind to complete stillness. If the mind were powered by electricity, contemplation would simply mean pulling the plug. To be utterly at rest is to know one's self in the state of shalom—the peace that "passes all understanding." In giving up all illusion about holding one's own self in being, one surrenders into "the everlasting arms." To desire nothing, to do nothing, to be nothing—that is the most honest and direct posture in terms of who one truly is. The gift is to feel one's life as gift, every moment, in each mysterious nook and cranny. Truly to be, is to be "home."

To open yourself to such experience, try to put yourself physically into a symbolic posture of this experience, one of emptiness and stillness, of humility wrapped in silence. Cash in all your "whys" for a simple "that." It is consciousness that will stand in your way. Self-consciousness is the awareness by an "I" of a "me." Consequently, every waking (and often sleeping) moment is consumed by the incessant chatter of the two, acting like teenagers at an overnight. It is in such silent noise that one spiritually suffocates. So why don't we stop it? Because we are afraid of what might happen if we did. Chattering is the inner noise that distracts us from confessing the lie we are living—that of being self-constituted, and thus needing nothing more than one's self. But to stop, to do nothing, to say nothing, even to be physically alone, brings the terrifying truth, of living a lie.

Yet even if the primal peace that is promised by this spirit mode does tempt us to stop for a moment, we don't know how. So what's the secret? The heart of the contemplative method is to give the mind something to play with, so as to keep it out of the way. A phrase used for so "dribbling" the mind is what tradition calls a mantra. The technique is simple, requiring only disciplined practice. Remember that the goal is to enter the abyss in a thoughtless state, as the quiet mind of a centered self.[4] This is how.

- Set aside a period of time, perhaps fifteen minutes as a start.
- Assume a restful, comfortable posture, in a quiet place where you are sure not to be disturbed.
- Let go, permitting the chair or floor to do all the supporting, and you none.
- Take slow, deep breaths, with an emphasis on exhaling, all the tensions, anxieties, concerns—blow them out one by one if necessary, perhaps by name. If you are particularly tense, begin with the toes and slowly "let go" as you work your way up the body, finally reaching the mind.
- Permit a word or phrase to emerge from your feelings, which will probably identify your present state. Let it function as your mantra. For example, a particularly hard day might suggest "Give me peace." Facing a trying week, one might find arising "Accept me as I am." Repeat it at the same speed as your own state of being. In times of stress, that will mean repeating it rapidly. The point is to say it just fast enough to demand the full attention of your mind. If you begin to think of anything other than the mantra, increase the tempo until the mind is brought back again to be consumed in the "drib-

bling." Normally the pace of repetition will slow on its own. Permit this slowing to happen, as long as thinking does not return. If it does, increase the pace, calling the mind back to what it promised to do during recess.

- Images will keep coming. This is of no concern. Simply let them pass by, without participating, much as one does with traffic while waiting patiently for a bus. If you see a mountain, look, but do not climb it. Pick up no rocks to examine them, and have no conversations with strangers. The nontask is not-to-seek. Simply observe, with growing disinterest and increasing passivity. The senses are darkening.

- Persist in literally doing nothing, but be gentle with yourself. Armed only with the spirit-chosen mantra, your whole being will begin to slow, grow quiet. As quality of being replaces in importance the flurry of content, you will experience a growing deepness. The mind preoccupied becomes increasingly indifferent to "this, not that," and "here, not there." Permit it to happen, without thinking about it. Even to name it is to make it an object about which to think, rather than a state in which to participate. The self must become pure subject, indifferent to the sideshow, confident that it too will pass.

- There will come a point when, without your awareness, even the mantra will pass. Everything stops, unaware of the stopping. You simply are, suspended motionlessly over nothingness, inside everything—and all is well. This is to rest at the Center, at the still point of the turning wheel, within the Mystery, embraced by the Creative Ground of all. Tranquillity. Contentedness. Peace. The inner joy of no separation. The final harbor. To be, truly.

- When the agreed-upon time is over, slowly let a feeling or word or image emerge, as self-consciousness is being reborn. Usually it comes gift-wrapped in thankfulness. It is yours, as a token for your pocket, until next time. Repeat it, savor the afterglow. Take it with you into the day—as a reminder of death and rebirth.[5]

Such contemplation may bring you several very special gifts. The first is a sixth sense, which can be called the capacity of the heart. It is the ability to see things and situations from within. A second is release from work addiction. Spirituality begins, Merton once said, when one can do nothing and feel no guilt. In literally doing nothing, there can be birthed a new state. Ironically, it

is the opposite of waste or boredom. But only experience can
teach that.

Experiment with variations within this exercise. For example,
hold your palms together. With your thumbs on your chin, press
your upright fingers against the center of your forehead, symbol-
izing the "third eye" or place of wisdom. This provides a physical
focus for centering. Some prefer a visual focus, such as a candle,
an icon, a painting, a blank piece of paper, a circle, a ball. Some
persons find helpful a list of words, to be reread until a particular
one suggests itself as focus. Begin a personal list, considering as
candidates such words as mystery, being, nothingness, abyss,
ground, depth, black hole, unfathomable, boundless, immeasur-
able.

2. *Om*

An "Om" was previously identified as the sound of sounds, of
everything from a child's "ah" to a lover's sigh. An Om is made by
breathing deeply several times, and then letting the breath out as
an "O." Halfway out of breath, permit it to turn toward an "H"
sound, finishing finally as an "M" that trails off into nothingness.
Do this a number of times, until one's lung cage feels totally full,
no empty places in one's body, and the self so tingles that one's
edges are without recognizable boundaries. Rest in the experience, imaging oneself as surrounded and invaded by the One in
whom one lives and moves and has one's being.

3. *Image Contemplation*

Once one has a taste for this mode, one can find various analogies helpful in evoking it. For example, image your breathing as
drawing God in and out of your life. Or image breathing as God
entering and leaving one's self, so that one's existence depends on
resting in and riding on the undulating Divine breath. Enter into
the image until one becomes it. Air itself, surrounding and invad-
ing every part of one's personhood, can image the ocean of Divine
Presence. Likewise, one's own thinking can image the mind of
God thinking one's self into being, holding one lovingly there
within the Imagination. It may be enough simply to hold a seed in
the palm of one's hand.

4. *Ravished by Silence*

The most powerful expression of this type may occur by going where one is invaded by a silence that "booms." This can be a monastery, the deep woods, a cemetery even in the city, a padded gymnasium after hours, floating on water, or swimming slowly underwater. One must find such a place, or die. The one requirement is that it be where you can close the door, in effect, breathe deeply, and say, "Finally." Wherever that is, it is "home."

5. *Changed Vantage Point*

This spiritual type can be experienced quickly by intentionally changing one's physical location. By lying on one's back, for example, even on a tenement roof, gazing at the stars on a moonless night, one's huge daily dilemmas are given a new perspective. Two introductory courses in such an approach are offered daily—at sunrise and at sunset. No preparation is needed, no tuition required. Just be there. The demonstrations are for those of us who feel responsible for the whole world. Amazingly, the world at such times takes fine care of itself, without need of consultation.

Take a siesta with the explicit thought of resting in God, being wrapped in the everlasting arms, rooted and grounded in peace. Taste it.

6. *Mystery*

Once tasted, mystery is beheld as residing in the fact of anything. Thus mystery is as available as every moment, within arm's reach. Several such moments come readily to mind. Grandparent and grandchild enjoying each other's presence. Looking deeply into the eyes of one you love. Savoring the feel of one's body when it is functioning well.

7. *Music*

This spirit mode is birthed in becoming lost in a piece of well-chosen music. Ironically this is difficult for many persons to experience, for music in our time has been squandered as background filler. As a result, it can be a unique experience to listen to a piece of music intentionally and thus intensely, for a set period of time, resisting all distractions. As T. S. Eliot knew, this mode can occur when "music [is] heard so deeply" that "you are the music."[6] My favorite music for this mode tends to be adagios. Some recordings easily available include François de Boisvallee's "Adagio Religioso," or Tomaso Albinoni's Adagio in G Minor. Debussy's *La Mer* is also a possibility, as is Wagner's Prelude to Act 3 of *Lohengrin*. In the end, however, the mystery characteristic of this spirit mode is probably best evoked by Gregorian chant.

8. *Paintings*

The visual person is helped by seeing what some of these spirit types might actually look like. Thus for each spirit mode certain paintings and painters whose work can serve as a focus of attention will be suggested. For such exercises, you might borrow or acquire a color-illustrated history of art, or a catalog of obtainable prints.[7] For this first spirit mode, Monet is a likely candidate. Almost any of his later paintings will do, such as his studies of water lilies. If pushed to choose one or two of his works, I suggest *Yellow Iris* or *Weeping Willow*.[8] Let yourself be taken into the lyric abstraction of such paintings, not looking for anything recognizable. Feel, instead, the liquid energy, the shimmering formlessness, the endless overflow, like a timeless event. Permit the swirl of such color to draw you in, until you become a mysterious participant. The focus is not mystery in general but generally the mystery—that grounds anything, and thus everything. In Monet, one tastes those strange hints of the more that is less, and of the less that conjures the More. Here mystery is in, and with, and under, and as.

A Summary

This first spirit type makes contact with the restlessness inevitable in all of us, until we find our rest in the One in whom our restlessness is grounded. This motionless journey descends down into the heart of the self—to where all lines intersect and one passes into God. Here I know that there is nothing closer to God than myself, while God as Ground is closer to me than I am to myself. Silence is a signal for the spot where the inside of me touches the inside of God. Solace is the result. Shalom.

Such spirituality comes for some persons with a recognition that the hidden mystery has a luminous Center. For others, it is like gazing into Nothingness and finding it intimate and friendly.

For still others, what is entailed feels more like a gamble. Gazing at the emptiness, armed with the aroma of hope, one trusts that one's yearning for the dark Silence is a token of having been found.

Evoking this spirit mode may take little more than imagining a billion light years, or pondering a solar system within the solar system of a solar system. However it occurs, the feel is of an Eternal Now which is a homecoming, a returning to the Source, where one's origin and the destiny of the cosmos are one. We come forth from God and we return to God, with mystery tied as bows on both ends. Thus the most honest of human gestures is to quiet both speech and thought. In that moment, without thinking or feeling or speaking, one simply is—in the Quietness as presence.

Some women theologians find this first mode to be an excellent feminist spirit base. What they find inadequate is not the experience but the traditional language. "Father-Creator" suggests, for them, "masculine" images of power and manipulation, with such analogies as maker, builder, or engineer. Thus they find metaphors drawn from feminine experience better able to rediscover this spirit type of Abyss experienced as Mystery.

> Every reasonable notion of time and space dissolves into a primordial pool that seems unfathomable. One is unable to imagine this beginningless beginning. . . . What lies beyond the first mother, whether we search our own experience or the vastness of the physical universe, still seems to be a kind of mother, something that accommodates all possible questions and sustains the birth and death of ideas and living beings. This mother of all things is groundless, without any identifiable source. . . . Originless fecundity. . . . This primordial, all-accommodating spaciousness is the fundamental quality of the feminine."[9]

The trinitarian spirituality we are describing under the three dimensions of God as Creator arises from three insatiable questions. The first we have explored: Why anything? It is to the other two that we now turn: Why this? (type 2), and What for? (type 3).

4

Serenity in the Abiding

Type 2: Order

Luther wisely insisted that a God understood as creative power alone would be malevolent, for without order the mysterious outpouring would be arbitrary and capricious. Therefore type 2 focuses on the ordering (Logos) of the God experienced in type 1 as Creative Ground. Sheer power without pattern is meaningless eruption, illustrated well by the fairy tale of the porridge pot that would not stop boiling over. The issue in this mode is not outcome but structure. The focus of this experience is the form of the abiding—in and with everything, giving a serene sense of purpose and reliability to the whole and to every part.

The Abiding as Faithful

I remember walking home after a bad day in grade school. Everything was in shambles. Nothing had gone as it should, not even recess. And there, in the middle of Miller Avenue, I stopped, looked around, and yelled, "Well, spring's coming, and you can't stop it!" That's what this type is about, the assurance of being shaped by faithful order. On the one hand, one marvels at the loyalty that gives to life a predictability. On the other, one becomes intoxicated by the shapes and gestalts that hold together each speck of existence, without exception.

The focus here is not on the form of *anything*, but the *form* of anything. It is pattern that fascinates, for its own sake, whether discerned in tea leaves, tiled roofs, car tracks in early snow, or deer trails on mountain tundra. Plato understood well this mode, recognizing in mathematics the ultimate expression of reality.

Numbers were for him a way of imaging life as rooted in an orderly foundation. Thus reality, requiring form simply to be, is, by its nature, universally intentional. While one's individual life seems arbitrary at times, life itself, as undergirding all arbitrariness, is experienced here as constant.

An illustration might help. For most persons, "gravity" is a scientific term that supposedly explains a phenomenon. Yet, if one thinks about it, "gravity" is simply a word that points without explanation to an incredible situation. Do you have a pencil in your hand? Open your fingers. What happened? It "fell." What does that mean? That it went down, not up or sideways. How did I know? That's the issue. There is absolutely no necessity in the pencil or the floor to make them come together as they did. But they did. What's more, it is my firm belief that the order binding everything is such that tomorrow, at 8 A.M., if you take that same pencil, and open your same fingers, it will happen again and again—the pencil will go down, not up. Next week too. If you find something astonishing about all that, you are on the edge of this second spirit type.

Echoes of the Eternal

Let's try again. In this mode, one becomes enchanted with the pregnancy of pure form. I remember my first encounter with a Japanese potter. Time after time he created near-perfect bowls of pure form. I was captivated by the constancy of shape. As I watched, it was as if his repetition of form was a timeless act, in which he became one with the earth, centered in perfect orbit around its own turning wheel. Great classical architecture hints of this same abidingness, as line and shape imitate the purity of circle, square, cube, or triangle. Such expressions tease and lure us, for they are hints and promises through geometric form of a perfection in which finite life participates but never attains.

I was captured by this spirit mode at the Great Pyramids at Giza, near Cairo. Riding the shifting sands from the vantage of a plodding camel, as on the horizon three faultless triangles were silhouetted against the evening sky—that is to become intoxicated by the eternal. Surrounded by a vast and silent serenity, one can almost imagine that each speck of sand has its sacred place and number. And in the original interior wall paintings of these same pyramids, form transforms apparent chaos into meaning—laying out everything in ordered cycles of events and days, seasons and years, dynasties and beyond. Inside and out, the "was" and "is" and "shall be" are ordered into an endless splendor of foreverness. In such a situation, life exudes a sculptured serenity, a contoured silence, a cosmic composure. Each of everything has its ordered place—all belongs, somewhere, everywhere, always. "For everything there is a season, and a time for every matter under heaven" (Eccl. 3:1).

An afternoon on the Acropolis, or staring at a piece of honeycomb—such are the times that give birth to a shy but melancholy longing that "somewhere" such purity must be, for it is now, almost. This mode tantalizes, holding us in a paradox, between the poles of hint and of insatiability. The "cannot be" tempts us with an "is" of a different order.

Pure form puts a claim on us, as having the right to be. One can sense this even in doodling, or fondling the smooth roundness of a stone, or drawing a line with a straight edge, or creating circles within circles with a compass, or accepting a child's invitation to play with her blocks. Spiders are the masters of this mode, weaving identical, gleaming webs in the morning sunlight. My special preference is for a giant harvest moon, calming the city's glitter as it floats motionless over the cluttered horizon. The gasp that one makes, in spite of oneself, is an expression of participating in creation's binding force.

The Form of Forms

Through such form, one senses a strange familiarity behind the unfamiliar. These are hints of homesickness for a "place" we have never been before. But if we haven't, why the melancholy? Yet in such moments one does feel like an exile, peeking through a window, but never invited in through the door. Something is being evoked that feels like a "memory," a strange recall of once being at home among that "abidingness" that belongs to the integrity of Form itself. It is almost as if there was a "once" when all was in relation and belonged, together. In fact, one can almost see through everything—and for a moment there is order, *now*, in which each thing has its place, and all makes sense, for everything fits. All is well, as one craves that it is truly so.

By this time one is beginning to have a "feel" for this spirit mode or it may always sound like babbling. Give me two minutes for one last try. Pick a dandelion. Stare at the incredible design of infinitesimal petals radiating as a common dome. Perhaps, just perhaps, by staring right at its middle, you can sense an intentionality, rationality, purpose, logos, pattern, essence. Call it what you will, one senses a serenity as final promise.

Plato developed this spirit type, in fact, into a full-fledged philosophy. Taking these experiences to their logical conclusion, he insisted that each type of everything exists because it participates in its own perfect, eternal form. A beautifully shaped Shaker table is radiant in its simplicity, for it approximates the sacred form of "tableness," as like inheres in Like for its meaning. So it is with the human soul, fashioned by One who has and gives through form an infinite worth.

Hay bales in monotonous pattern, fence posts in deadly repetition—there hardly appears to be much there. Yet in intuiting the pattern that holds such common things together, perhaps by moonlight, one is grasped by an uncommon serenity. Before one's gaze everything stops, baptized as the monumental, the "always has been." For a moment, the relentless deterioration of time stops, in an eternal now.

From this perspective, it is possible to understand religion itself as the form of forms, the order of orders, the center of centers, the patterned hub of the turning wheel, the liturgy of a perfect triangle. The intent of the catechism, then, is to form each person by the mind of Christ. So formed, worship becomes a rehearsal of the form structuring the cosmos as plot. Here Logos becomes the name for Christ—as exhibiting the Form of God and thus being the One in whom "all things hold together" (Col. 1:17).

Need and Heresy

What claims us in this spirit mode, then, is the underlying "unchangingness" of reality—the unmoving form of even movement itself, the abiding and faithful loyalty holding together everything, from cosmos to electron. As we noted in chapter 2, the hymnist understands: "We blossom and flourish as leaves on the tree,/and wither and perish, but naught changeth thee" ("Immortal, Invisible, God Only Wise").[1]

The first spirit mode we explored, focused in mystery, has a special affinity with Eastern theology. Western theology, on the other hand, is deeply immersed in this second mode, tending to define both cosmos and God in terms of form or essence. So much has this been the case that classic Western theology has declared God to be the form of Forms, and thus the Unmoved Mover. Here, in encountering the danger of this spirit mode, we recognize the temptation present in every mode: to claim it as exclusive. Since this spirit type tended to predominate in medieval Christianity, the tendency was to identify God's perfection exclusively in terms of changelessness. As a result, everything that changes was regarded as "fallen," so much so that even change itself and thus the world were often seen as being ultimately unreal.

Ironically, the danger today is a "heresy" born of the opposite exclusivity. Our modern intoxication with change tends to undercut this second spirit mode, leaving unfed the human hunger for that serenity which belongs to the abiding.

Here we can appreciate the implications of the pluralistic spirituality we are developing. The mode we are considering does *not* mean pitting order against change. Rather, the focus is on the order *undergirding* change. In contrast, our culture is on the verge of losing itself in the trap of change for its own sake. Parabolic is the pilgrimage of the architect Le Corbusier. His career was transformed by visiting the Great Plains. Here he found an uncommon beauty in the ordered pattern of poured-concrete grain elevators. As he gazed on them, they became serene monuments of pure form on the earth's tabletop. May the play paraphernalia of every child never be deprived of building blocks.

Stopping to See

This experience of abidingness remains available, even in this time of rapid change, for those who know how to look. There is the weathered barn, seen from the interstate as it stands silhouetted against a winter sky, outlasting its builders. Even in the smog, birds continue to fly south, in a formation they have always flown. Telephone poles stretching along a Montana road in infinite regress sing the refrain. And contoured patterns of spring plowing on a brown and gentle hillside are still an invitation to bare feet.

It is startling how many of us today are fearful of the stillness defining this mode. It is as if by stopping our dogged activities "life" would stop. It is as if we can trust only that modicum of order which each individual is able to gain momentarily by clutching. In contrast, we need, and are blessed, by those who still trust in another Order. To still the weary heart, to hone the world to a fine point, to put down roots for an anchorage, to make commitments that promise to outlast time, to feel one's heart caught at the apex of a dancer's leap, to die a million deaths in praying for the infinite suspension of a special moment—these are the tidbits of life fit only for an Eternity. Within such ordered moments the habits of the heart are forged. And, as creatures of habit, we cannot rest until we have sensed in Creator, and thus Creation, those correlative habits of the heart, as faithfulness.

EXERCISES

1. *The Jesus Prayer*

This practice, drawn from the resources of the Russian Church, consists of repeating one sentence, over and over again, until one's consciousness is permanently formed by its repetitive pattern. An analogy is the tendency of the first song one hears in the morning to linger throughout the day, singing itself almost imperceptibly yet indelibly. Analogous is a melody by which one becomes haunted, which can be removed only by replacement. This is the strategy behind advertising jingles on the radio.

Such a practice signals that spirit life is far more than occasional activity. Thus Paul insisted that one should pray constantly, in all circumstances (1 Thess. 5:17). This seemingly impossible goal becomes realistic, however, when an unceasing activity of one's body becomes reshaped by correlation with prayer words. This is possible by repeating the Jesus Prayer to the ordered rhythm of one's breathing, or to one's heartbeat. Thus one breathes in while saying, "Lord Jesus Christ," and breathes out with the words, "Have mercy on me." This correlation becomes ingrained by regular periods of disciplined repetition—in the shower, the car, waiting for an appointment, before going to sleep, while dressing in the morning. Through such repetition, associating one's breathing or heartbeat with repeated words, one's body begins to pray without ceasing, becoming a "temple" of intentional form.[2]

2. *Habit*

We are creatures of habit. Each of us has a favorite chair, food, expression, song—a favorite almost everything. We take the same route to work or even the store, develop a characteristic walk, eat what is on our plate in the same sequence, sit in the same pew, keep a favorite piece of clothing long after it deserves decent burial, and order at a restaurant "the usual." These habits serve as hints that we are congenitally defined by pattern. If any of these habits is interrupted, we become disoriented. And by exercising them, our meaning is restored. Because such repetition is so powerful, it can take on the power of superstition, if not magic. Nonetheless, an axiom presents itself: to forge habits by disciplined, self-conscious repetition is to change, solidify, and/or deepen one's orientation in meaning.

One effort by the medieval church at such a spirituality of intentional ordering was the Angelus. This triune prayer was repeated when the village church bell rang, wherever one happened to be—at morning, noon, and evening. A modern equivalent would be to memorize a simple prayer to be said every hour on the hour, when one's digital watch makes its sound.

Since repetition characterizes most portions of our life, do an appraisal of the primary ones informing your daily life. Every eating is followed by a hungering, every going entails a return, every rising a sleep, every dressing an undressing. Such are the repetitions capable of becoming meaningful acts. Once they are identified, appropriately modified if necessary, and claimed with words, they become common-day act-liturgies. The comfort of meaningful repetition evokes trust because, recognized or not, it mirrors the Order to which life belongs.

My favorite way of renewing this spirit mode is a Sunday morning walk in the downtown section of "my" city. Everything is stopped, with a rare and serene order—empty streets, skyscrapers with a verticalness once reserved for plumb lines, banisters in orderly parade, and the shadows of fire escapes painting the sidewalks and streets with geometry.

Protestants often distain Roman Catholics for the "nonsense" of their varied practices in this mode, such as repeating the rosary. Yet I can still identify each one of my relatives by the characteristic prayer each would always repeat when offering "table grace." In fact, I still find solace in using for grace the identical words my father used for eighteen years at our family table. And I must confess that I have memorized the rosary, finding its repetitive phrases helpful in calming times of crisis—crisis means "to separate" from the normal order.

Litany is a prayer form made to order for this spirit mode. For each supplication there is a fixed response. A powerful rehearsal to encourage one's originality here is to read aloud Psalm 136. After each statement of Divine action, there comes, twenty-six times, this refrain, "For [God's] steadfast love endures for ever."

Try repeating such a litany in the same place, with identical posture, at the same time, on the same day of the week, while wearing the same special article of clothing.

3. *Focused Meditation*

For some, entering this mode takes little more than drumming one's fingers, staring at a triangle drawn on a piece of paper, becoming mesmerized by the digital precision of one's computer, cutting a carrot or an apple in cross section and studying the design, or looking at anything microscopically.

While one needs to prepare one's own list from which to draw for meditation, it might include such words as essence, form, order, dependability, intentionality, faithfulness, predictability, constancy, structure, shape, pattern, changelessness, solidarity, and integrity.

4. *Simplicity*

We are all pack rats, differing only in quantity. In fact, such a tendency may be a clue to obesity—surrounding one's self with quantity sufficient to pad oneself against vulnerability. Thus an act of intentional vulnerability can be an important spirit experience. I recall indelibly from boyhood the annual liturgy called "spring housecleaning." It was a shadow of Israel's ideal of jubilee, when everything was restored to the simplicity of equality and justice. The practice of observing every seventh day as the restoration of each person was echoed in giving rest to the fields every seventh year. And after "seven times seven years," the trumpet shall sound and "proclaim liberty" as "a jubilee for you" (Lev. 25:8–17). Property was then restored to its rightful owner, people returned home, and life began over again—new. In the case of my family, the spring "jubilee" entailed giving away what we had accumulated that was unneeded to those who needed it. Everything left was washed, sorted, discarded, or salvaged. Each thing that survived this "simplicity review" was given its special and sacred place of belonging.

A less-demanding exercise would entail setting aside an afternoon to simplify an important place in or piece of your life, giving to it the integrity of simple order. Particularly for those of us who tend toward defensiveness by cluttering, a fine spiritual act is to simplify one's life so as to reduce the whole to its fundamentals.[3]

5. *Seasons*

The death of the family farm is not only its own tragedy, but marks the loss to the communities of many persons who by vocation were furrowed naturally by this spirit mode. People of the soil survive by knowing by heart the cycles of life and death, growth and harvest, work and leisure. The seasons forge deep sensitivity for an abiding and ordering reliability beneath it all. The oft-heard characterization of farmers as "conservative" may reflect a sensitivity, honed by a monasticlike endurance, for cycled sameness as a serene liturgy. Modern society air-conditions the summer and heats the winter, levels the hills and fills the valleys into a gray sameness, purging real order of significant anticipation.

Therefore, depending on where you live, discover ways in which to participate in seasonal transitions. For me, nothing substitutes for walking the prairies as the cold north wind announces the earth's hibernation. There are the Ozark dogwoods, declaring spring with reckless abandon. And the New England of my educational years so forged my memory of fall that Connecticut would not dare to begin the process without me.

6. *Music*

Johann Sebastian Bach understood the musical forms he used as themselves an expression of this spirit experience. Thus his final masterpiece, the *Art of the Fugue*, brought to pure expression the form which for much of his life bore witness to the Divine order behind all movement. In mathematical-like resolution, the complexity of contrapuntal themes is resolved as independent but related melodies forming a fundamental harmony—a final resolution reflective for him of the triune God. Sensing death coming, he stopped his final fugues at midpoint, wrote the choral prelude "Before Thy Throne I Stand," and died—into that perfect order, the promise of which he had experienced as foretaste through the rarified form of music.

A powerful exercise in this spirit mode, then, is to listen repeatedly to his *Art of the Fugue*. Especially moving is an authentic version that stops abruptly in mid-phrase. Any of Bach's "toccata and fugues" will do nicely. Appropriately, a toccata is a free-style composition, used as prelude to the carefully ordered resolution characteristic of a fugue. Pachelbel's Canon in D is a composition particularly available for many persons.

It is possible that the heavy drivenness of repetitive beat in rock music expresses latently this mode. In fact, the universal love of music is understandable if one recognizes music as the form of forms. The love of pulsing, throbbing rhythm is the more blatant hunger for a pattern that can redeem life into ritual. I used to be irritated by the unimaginative words of current music, in which a simple, inane sentence is sung, over and over again, without development or even variation. I believe I missed the point of its appeal.

7. *Daily Worship*

There is no culture that does not give form to the rhythm of the day, the months, the seasons of the year, the years of a lifetime, the epochs of a race, the expansion and return of the cosmos. While we will refer more in detail to this characteristic in another spirit mode, an important exercise here is the conscious effort to identify which of these patterns have taken on elevated significance in your life. One's weekly pattern, one hopes, will rest on more than the collapse identifiable as "Thank God it's Friday." The popularity of devotional booklets like *Upper Room* as devotional resources rests in large part in their providing a rhythmic pattern for beginning or ending one's day.

8. *Form*

Visit a Shaker village or a workshop where handmade furniture is made. In fact, almost any craftsperson will do, one who recognizes the honest shaping of authentic material as an art form. Here an integrity touching the spiritual is nurtured. Ask to fondle the wood, the shape, the form as it captures function. If there is a Frank Lloyd Wright house in your area, visit it as a spiritual act. If not, visit his Fallingwater home in Pennsylvania as a special pilgrimage.

Thomas Merton used a camera for immersing himself in this spirit mode. Look at a collection of his pictures, noting particularly how much they are pictures of forms that suggest the abiding. Borrow a camera, if you do not have one, and find those "moments" whose significance are worth stopping. I would not care if you forgot the film. After all, a camera is only a reminder of how to look, exercising one's ability to see what one expects.

Each family has traditions—realized or unrealized, valued or resented. Meet with members of your immediate or extended family. How many such "rituals" can you name? Which of them are worth preserving? Which deserve to be forgotten, or even atoned for with others? Where are there gaps in the overall rhythm that does or can hold your family together? If necessary, write these down and share them by correspondence. Notice how fascinated grandchildren are with stories of "the way it used to be." Don't simply tell them. Restore them by recruiting the children as major participants. After all these years, what I recall as perhaps my first taste for liturgy had to do with grandmother's sugar cookies and cold milk on the way home from school.

Take a course or participate in a continuing education event in ceramics. At the very least, find a potter who will let you center a piece of clay on the wheel. There may be no better action-parable for what life is about.

9. *Painting*

A carefully chosen painting as an object for meditation is a helpful exercise in each spirit type. In the type we are exploring, Cézanne is master.[4] His advice to aspiring painters was to discern everything in terms of cones, squares, spheres, and cylinders. Consider any of his paintings of Mont Sainte-Victoire. He painted and repainted this one mountain, so craving to distill one thing into its purest form that one passes beyond particularity into the inner structure that holds everything intentionally together. As he persevered, painting after painting, concreteness continued to fade into a translucence of form. The naked givenness of canvas was even permitted to extrude, as he increasingly used faded earth colors to convey the ancient and eternal. Whether painting nature, villages, or persons, Cézanne's fascination was with the elementary and inclusive forms that bind life together in meaning. He sought for that which joins a face, a bowl of fruit, a mountain into that monumental depth in which all belong to the abiding. His is the ability to bring us into the presence of a fabric of timeless, unagitated, common order, at a depth which is for its own sake. In this spirit type, what one senses is the tension of being "in but not of," while being "of but not in."

A Summary

What emerges in this spirit mode is a wisdom born of serene-
ness, an ordered rightness hinting of that which has always been.
The modern lament over the cheap shabbiness of present-day
products is a sense of loss for emblems sufficient to evoke such
spirituality. The self cannot long retain integrity in a world shaped
by planned obsolescence. The destruction of every constant, the
relativizing of each absolute, and the loss of any givenness beyond
subjectivity—these are the marks of a worn autonomy out of
which is being born a frantic hunger for this spirit mode in our
time.

Paul, in his letter to the Colossians, uses the language of this
mode for understanding the second member of the Trinity. Christ
is the "image of the invisible God," creation's firstborn, the Logos
in whom all things are created. "In heaven and on earth, visible
and invisible, . . . all things were created through him and for
him." In so being, Christ is the spatio-temporal interface through
which "all things hold together" (Col. 1:15–17). It is as the Form
of forms that Christ is revelation, giving intentional pattern
(Logos) to the "Abyss" as promise.

Paul declares this Logos to be the fullness that reconciles, for
this pattern of beginning and ending (type 2) has in Jesus Christ
become the fullness of form Incarnate (type 5), to be experienced
expansively as an embracing sacramentalism (type 8). So expressed, we have an anticipation of the Trinity of Manifestation.

5

Rhythm
and the Restless Voyage

Type 3: Becoming

Everything that exists is bottomless (type 1), and is held in being by form (type 2). But there is also a third givenness characterizing all that is—a "not-yet-ness." One can experience this as a pervading restlessness flapping at all the edges—a vital, dynamic energy surging, pervading and thrusting everything into motion and becoming. This ecstatic impulse, which we call the Spirit as Creator, appears in the first verses of Genesis. Brooding over the face of the Abyss, God creates by roving ceaselessly to and fro. And so, deep within us, this same brooding of spirit is to be experienced. This is where the midnight restlessness meets its Cause.

Even in its unthinking state, this insatiability goads the imagination, luring the artist in each of us into countless fantasies of possibility. The mind, the unconscious, the doodling fingers, the tapping toes—all in motion, so that one is led to suspect that what is motionless is dead. Life itself is animation, as every part participates irresistibly in the Rhythm of rhythms. The beat goes on, inflaming passion into dance. Thus, says Nietzsche, "I could believe only in a God that would know how to dance."

The Pulsing Creativity

The "feel" of this mode is readily available. One finds it in the pulsing undulation of ripe grain, the restless choreography of a spring thunderstorm, the flutter and bowing in fall of aspen leaves in full sunlight, the persistence of clouds dusting snow from mountain peaks. In fact, this may be the easiest spirit mode for our restless, ever-moving generation to sense.

As we get closer to nature on vacation, rare is the person who is not fascinated by the endless flowing of brook or waterfall. But it is the ocean that provides the classic expression. Here, in ceaseless sight and sound, one is so caught up in the motion that one becomes the motion—not the motion *of* something, but the motion *as* motion. No beginning. No ending. Forever. And while we never "arrive" anywhere, strangely in the movement itself we are at home. The dance is for the dancing. No wonder Saint John Damascene, or John of Damascus, referred to God as the "infinite ocean of being."

Pure Sound and Sight

For some, this spirit type finds its deepest welcome in music, particularly of the romantic tradition. Music, by its very nature, requires a time signature, assuring that there is a movement. Motion or no motion is never negotiable in music, only the pace. So it is in life. Music is noise redeemed and blessed, with even its divisions called movements—luring and lilting both the unconscious and the conscious into emergence. Even after the physical sound has ended, the soundless sound keeps on and on—inside. Viewed scientifically, sound waves go on forever. A song sung is for always.

Everywhere in nature one finds the sound of this mode. The wind serves well as illustration—rousing a spring shower, whispering through summer cedars, tumbling autumn leaves, roaring with driving snow. Caught up in this carnival of motion, with a sideshow at each corner, one can imagine the Spirit as "barker," empowering and orchestrating the whole to overflowing. The focus is on the Creator as restless impulse—pushing and luring each fragment toward its own special fullness. In so doing, the sails of the cosmos are filled for the relentless voyage of becoming. What is experienced in his mode is not goal but process, not arrival but movement, not content but dance.

Thomas Hardy wished the size of a village never to exceed the ability of a butterfly to fly in one end and out the other. Yet each of these first three spirit types we have been considering can be evoked by the urban world as well. Capturing the first might be the mystic power of a city after midnight, as it prepares to toss and turn its way to sleep. Illustrative of the second are the colored patterns of downtown lights on wet pavements after an evening shower. For the third, there is the addictiveness of the city's morning dance, as the serpentine flow of the interstate traffic feeds a waking and hungry metropolis. And one should never forget the eagerness of opening night—anywhere, of anything.

The Body's Dance

A perfect participation in this mode would be a giddy self-experience of the body as the elegant synchronic dance that it is. This would mean quivering to the speeding electrons of each part, becoming the tender balance of corpuscles and enzymes, the sloshing systole and diastole of the heart's chambers, the restless persistence of wind through lungs—everywhere the song of death and rebirth as syncopated and pulsating and amazing melody. So the universe. So God.

For some, the heart of religion is captured by defining its task as the sacralizing of space and time. Not long after conception, the womb became for each of us an intimate space defined by the beat and sounds of time. Surrounded by gurglings and murmurings and rumblings and ripplings, there is inflow through the relentless beat of a mother-heart, bigger than the embryo itself, while overhead the cavern echoes with the oceanlike rhythms of the lung's resolute breathing. It is no wonder, then, that birth as sudden exile leads directly into life as pilgrimage, searching for a beat and rhythm by which one might skip "home."

I am intrigued by teenagers. At a time in their lives when, supposedly, they are difficult to motivate, inclined to resist work, and refuse to become serious about much, they give serious meaning to their lives by being shaped in music and dance. They study to sound, walk the streets with ghetto blasters on full, and dance the weekends as if they had found a special sale on energy. Why? Perhaps they are less inhibited parables of the rest of us. Awkwardly restless as individuals, they find meaning in becoming lost in movement and sound. It makes sense, then, that religion centers in liturgy—where through movement and sound one participates in the rhythms by which the grounding Spirit is known as Holy.

This pulsing of the human spirit outward into the whole cosmos makes contact with the "new physics." In quantum theory, matter is recognized as not solid at all, but constituted by energy fields orchestrated in constant flux and change. The movement of the whole occurs in every part, and each energy particle displays the movement of the whole. One of the gifts of science is the discovery that even a piece of granite is, in Whitehead's words, "a rage of motion." And this is what the Christian doctrine of the Holy Spirit as Creator images well.[1]

Somehow, far back in my mind, this spirit type gets tied to a childhood memory—of experiencing a kite bobbing and soaring as it tugged on the end of my string.

EXERCISES

1. *Carnal Spirituality*

One of Christianity's greatest sins is its tendency to pit spirit against body, and then call the tension temptation. I recall that even at the age of twelve I was still asking myself how the minister got his children. Knowing how children were conceived, how could one ever believe that a person of God would have anything to do with such activities? Although I was embarrassed by Song of Solomon in the Bible, I would sneak peeks when my mother was out of the house. And I had no idea of what to make out of Paul's recognition of the sexual relationship as powerful analogy for the relation of Christ to the church, using language of bridegroom and body.

Therefore, an important exercise for each Christian is to make love to the glory of God. For this, one needs to create a context that deliberately forces the blending of the so-called secular and religious. If you have trouble understanding what I am suggesting, put a picture of Jesus on your bed stand before doing this "exercise." Dare you play "religious" music on the stereo and read scripture as a beginning? Let yourself feel deeply the surge of desire, the preparations, the ache, the longing, the arousing, the waves of moreness, the sensuality of every part, the choreography of body, the elasticity of time, the rhythm of body and breathing, the sounds, the smells, the crescendo, the union, the afterglow, the peace. Experience it all as an act of participating in God as Creative Spirit.

For those uneasy about relating earthly sexual patterns with spirituality, some reading from Teresa of Avila is helpful. She speaks of raptured "marriage" with God, and of sensual climax for "the divine Companionship within." Saint John of the Cross wrote poetry as a way of capturing his love affair with God. Some of his characteristic phrases are these: "Sick with love I am."

"Save only if of thee I have my fill." "Now blooms our nuptial bed." "Of my beloved drink I deep indeed." "Wounded by my glance that on thee play'd."[2] For him, the love affair of the Father's Son with the Spirit occurs within each of us, just as the Spirit's tender lovemaking with Mary provided redemption for the whole earth.

Because sexuality and spirituality interplay deeply and inevitably, one can understand why the church so quickly identified the misuse of the sensual as a spiritual offense. But it is the positive side of such attention that needs expression in our time, in a determined attempt to reclaim creatively the sensual as spiritual.

The sensual is broader than the sexual. Each of the senses is a powerful spiritual vehicle. How could it be otherwise when Christianity insists on Incarnation as the fleshly result of the Spirit's workings? Only a lack of focused imagination can limit the exercises possible within this spirit mode.

Take a ball of clay, and, with a sense of limitless time, play with it. Pat it, push into it, shape it, let it shape itself, form and touch it into being. Have water available for the fingers, to smooth and stroke its texture. Have nothing in mind. Do not make anything. If something emerges, so be it. If it remains a piece of clay in all its convoluting disguises, so be it. This spirit mode is known in the experience, not in the result.

Navahos ignite cedar chips as a way of combining senses with movement in praying. One may do the same with incense, as smell and the ascending visual spiral question horizontal predictability. Such upward dissolution is its own special dance into the eternal.

My first experience of a Trappist walk was disconcerting. I had always walked for utilitarian reasons to get exercise or to get somewhere. It was a means to an end. This time, when I accepted an invitation by the abbot, we walked down the lane. After a while, we gradually slowed, came to a tentative stop, and even more slowly turned back toward where we began—only to repeat the act, beginning again to stroll out the same lane—only to return, several times. We went nowhere, and everywhere, ending only when it ended itself, back where we began. The meaning was in the movement, with walking being for its own sake. Instead of taking a walk, a walk took us.

Relatedly, I was given a monastic cup as a gift. It is characterized by two handles. Drink with two hands and eyes closed, I was instructed, so that you will not be tempted to do two things at once. Ever since, that cup has been a reminder of this spirit mode: to participate fully in the rhythm of whatever is immediately before you. Kierkegaard understood: "Purity of heart is to will one thing." My "advanced" lesson in applying this perspective came in learning to wash dishes monastically. For the first time in my life, the washing was not to get them done. Instead, the joy was simply in the act of washing, sloshing and splashing for its own sake, until I too was part of the washing.

Once one gets the idea of experiencing an activity for its own sake, countless exercises will suggest themselves. Take any act that is immediately before you, and participate fully in its rhythm. Even the flow of writing with a pen can become a spiritual happening; and the simple act of reading, transposing moving sight into soundless sound, is an act stuffed with its own special "magic."

The word "sport" is short for "disport," whose root is "to carry." Something of its original meaning persists in talking of how a person "carries" himself or herself. An important exercise consists of becoming aware of how one does, in fact, carry oneself in simple gestures. Each of us is characterized by these: the toss of head, the manner of walk, the gestures of hands. Yet our friends rather than we ourselves tend to know what these are, and even what they may mean. The goal of this exercise is to recognize as many of these gestures as you can, and then to render some of them more "pure." That is, instead of "carrying" oneself in manners forged long ago by habit, competition, compensation, and unconscious imitations, modify them so that they become revealing motions of your real self, in fact or in hope. Working with a friend is helpful. Among your first efforts at transformation, consciously act out physically your immediate feelings—facially, and in walking, sitting, shaking hands. After some practice at that, try acting out your repressed and deprived feelings. How one walks down a hall, in gait and positioning in space, is a statement of inner being. With practice, one can gain a nurturing unity of feeling and act through motion. The two are interactive. One's being is expression in act; one's acting, in turn, is the nurturer of one's being.

The church has long used gestured movements for spiritual deepening—such as stretching forth hands over a chalice in blessing, or praying with cupped palms like begging bowls, or kneeling in humility, or prostrating oneself in Good Friday submission, or turning one's face "heavenward" as if in expectancy of a spring rain, or raising one's arms in invitation to the Spirit. Body communication is a wordless spirit-drama. After one spends time practicing such gestures, even the raising of a finger can become an exercise in the mystery of movement.

We often destroy "sport" as a spiritual activity by confusing it with competition. But if it means "to carry," this meaning can be related to any activity. Here the "feel" of the spiritual wraps itself around any near-perfect motion: the ball well hit, the cello well played, the mile well run, the pie well made. Each of us needs to identify, or learn, at least one activity that brings joy simply in its "well doing."

In no way need this mean being the best. It means doing one's best, or at least one's better. Two activities might serve me well here. One is swimming. Buoyed up and stroked by water, one can become enfolded in rhythm, stroke after stroke, at one with the breathing and the heartbeat and the roll of body. A second is jogging. When one settles in, the pace takes on an all-consuming liturgy of rhythm, even to the wind in one's hair. In either activity, one learns as spiritual the rhythmic grace of the long-distance runner. On a clear day, one can run forever. There is particular beauty in two persons doing such activities in rhythm together. I remember still the beauty of my twin daughters in high school as they ran the mile together, stride for stride, always crossing the finish line together.

Even competitive sports are spiritually redeemable. Golf can be played not to beat someone, but to do better than one has done before. A day for special remembrance is "the time I shot a 70!" Trying for one's "personal best" is a goal that can keep flowing back to purify any doing.

Team sports have spiritual possibilities as well, if modified. In volleyball, for example, rotate the whole court, instead of rotating only each side. Thus in scoring one point, a player might be playing on one side of the net, while for the next she might be on the opposite side. One might be trying a spike against one person on one play, only to be setting up a play for that same person on another serve. When the game is "won," there is no winner and no loser, no "we versus them." The fun is in the movement itself, of both winning and losing, as the playing is for its own sake.

A letter from my daughter visiting the Florida Keys seems promising as an exercise in this spirit type:

> Snorkeling off a coral reef is unbelievable. For starters, floating ef-

fortlessly and breathing while under water in the warm waters of the ocean is like being in the womb of the Earth herself. And the life forms under the surface have no parallel on dry land. It is like looking at things from the inside. Billions of kinds of coral, and the most ridiculously exotic fish in truly unbelievable colors—yellow and purple stripes, neon-blue polka dots, always moving, like punk rockers of the deep. Incredible. But permeating it all are the ocean's currents, making everything—coral fans, fish, and you—rock back and forth in this hypnotic rhythm.

I'll keep that one on hold for a while, along with my yearnings to fly a sailplane, or even a hot-air balloon, on a Sunday afternoon. You try them. My own favorite version is inner-tubing the rapids. Actually, this spirit type requires little more than stepping into any motion. I still remember as a child wading in the tug and tickle of a stream. As a teenager, it involved the experience of rising and descending, just beyond where the ocean waves break. And today I still "have that thing" about wind in my hair.

2. Meditation

There are words useful for meditating on this spirit mode. As a beginning for your collection, consider these: restlessness, energy, surge, dance, movement, yearning, rhythm, insatiability, expansiveness, animation, fervor, irresistibility, appetite.

3. Focus

It is possible to become mesmerized by expressions of this spirit mode. What is it about a grandfather clock that causes one to be entranced by the perpetual motion of a pendulum? Even as an energetic child, I respectfully stopped to watch every time I visited my uncle. Then there is the sacred art of fire-watching. It takes only a fireplace, one match (two for some of us), some kindling, two logs, a pillow, and endless time.

The novelist Herman Melville painted with words in a manner particularly sensitive to this spirit mode, often focusing on water. In *Moby Dick*, Ishmael discovers that when life overwhelms one badly, it is "high time to get to sea." Every sea town, he muses, is arranged so as to move the "crowds of water gazers" waterward. There is something about water that evokes a deepness for this spirit mode.

Say you are in the country; in some high land of lakes. Take almost any path you please, and ten to one it carries you down in a dale, and leaves you there by a pool in the stream. There is magic in it. . . . Yes, as every one knows, meditation and water are wedded for ever.[3]

Magic? Melville pushes toward spirit: "We ourselves see in all rivers and oceans . . . the image of the ungraspable phantom of life; and this is the key to it all."[4] That "ungraspable phantom" goes by the name Spirit, experienced as Creator.

Saint Jerome understood this, recognizing that it is the triune Spirit so experienced that answers the question, "When shall I go and see the face of God?" Our thirst for God is for "the living fountain," a "fountain of water, springing up into eternal life." As the deer longs for running water, so one's soul longs for the racing Spirit. Thus it is in baptism by water and by Spirit, three times captured through one's immersion into the movement of burial and resurrection, that one comes to know "the three fountains of the Church constitut[ing] the mystery of the Trinity."[5]

4. *Music*

To become lost in the flowing and soaring of romantic music has no equal in touching this mode. For those unfamiliar with such possibilities, Ravel's *Bolero* is a piece within the reach of most persons. Assume the most comfortable position possible. Listen with openness, letting one's body repeat the rhythm in any way it might choose for you. Here one can taste that relentless persistence which only the beat of the heart can emulate. Such music so fastens itself within one's being that even when it is over, one savors the silence itself as rhythmic.

Two other possibilities are Liszt's Hungarian Rhapsody No. 1 and Brahms's Hungarian Dance No. 5.

5. *Dance*

I have never been able to overcome fully the impact of having been raised in a family where dancing was considered immoral. My substitute has been music, with a touch of envy when I attended a ballet. But if music can so "move" my feelings, what would it be like if I could get out of the way and let it bring *me* to movement? The phenomenon of dance, known in every culture, originates always as a spiritual ritual. It is understandable, then, why some persons suspect satanic influences behind the contagious power of rock music to lure one to dancing. Positively or negatively, movement shapes us in spiritual meanings, long before the lips can shape the sounds into faltering words.

I confess that I understand the importance of this exercise better than I can do it. My own feeble attempts at dancing require that I be alone, certain of not being seen. It may sound strange, but I find it helpful to read Psalm 150 before beginning: "Praise [God] with timbrel and dance" (Ps. 150:4). I follow this with playing a record with a contagious beat, perhaps that of some African American spiritual singers such as the O'Neal Twins, Willie Mae Ford Smith, or Mahalia Jackson.[6] Clapping usually comes naturally, and I experiment with "upbeat" and "downbeat" clapping. Beyond that, my advice is to myself as well as to you. Sway with the music. Rock from side to side. Use upraised arms, flexible hands, fluttering fingers. Take plenty of space, from living room to kitchen and back. Experience joy in sheer movement, in the fact that body and Spirit belong finally together. There may be a time, perhaps, when I can do what David felt compelled by joy to do—he danced naked before the Lord.

Music belongs to no one particular spirit mode. The issue is the choice of music, for there can be evocative offerings for each type. For example, the difference between type 2 and type 3 is simply illustrated: I have never felt the need to dance to a Bach fugue.

6. *Painting*

Van Gogh was so able to unite painter and painting that internal and external restlessness merged as a mutual belonging.[7] His eyes interacted with everything—stroking it, teasing it, pushing it, pleading with it, luring it—to become what it yearned to be. He painted everything, as if able to dab even the inanimate with hope—cafés, fields, trees, star-spangled nights. Such imagination created pictures in which even his bedroom glowed with color, as if an act of lovemaking. "May it not be," van Gogh wrote to his brother, "that one can perceive a thing better and more accurately by loving it?" Love is that passion which merges "spirits" in Spirit, a bubbling forth to overflowing, a form-bursting formlessness. He fondled color as if it were life's own energy. The excitement that swept through him came by participating in becoming—not becoming this or that, but becoming for its own sake. Such becoming, intertwining him with the revolutionary heart of Being as a restless and consuming dance, may have become "too much." He died at his own hands.

The spiritual gift bequeathed by such a painter is the ability to see what no brush can contain—a spring meadow, for starts. In such a place, everything is in buzzing motion, as if in flight: making ingress, outreaching, upturning, down-sweeping, waving and touching and expanding. In the rising heat waves, even the hills practice their own special dance step. The psalmist understood:

> " 'These are God's children'
> and while they dance they will sing:
> 'In you all find their home' "
> (Ps. 86:6–7, Paulist [Hebrew, 87:6–7]).

Another translation probes deeper:

> Singers and dancers alike say,
>   "All my springs are in you" (RSV).

One might not be surprised, then, that this spirit type can be grasped not only in certain paintings, but also through the technique by which they were created. So it is in Jackson Pollock's "action painting." With a huge canvas covering the floor, he moved the paint—dripping, throwing, smearing, pouring, whatever he in turn was moved to do. Being and doing became one, in a fierce kind of Dionysian dance, where artist and paint and expression merged in a spiritually organic action. Each "work" made claim to a name only later (for example, *Reflection on the Big Dipper*, or *Eyes in the Heat II*). Perhaps a child understands this process best.

A Summary

The image which this spirit type brings to my mind is that of a silent hawk riding the currents of the upper air. If asked for a second image, I would probably choose the earth at dawn, in its daily Te Deum of awakening, as life overflows its channels in insatiable sound. In type 1, we became lost in mystery, at the still point of its center. In type 2, we were claimed by the patterned serenity of eternal form. And here, in type 3, one sways to the rhythm of becoming. It is in such moments that one knows everything to be beyond the possibility of ever being finally formed or stilled or completed. Motion is the ingression in all that is, from atomic structure to the infinite expansion of the exploding universe itself.

All is dance. The trees clap their hands and God takes delight, for the Spirit *is* God—in, with, by, for, through—becoming, always.

A Look Back and Forward—Without Coffee

I have insisted that each of these spirit types, once clarified and rehearsed, can be recognized anywhere. It is time to illustrate this in summary with the first three modes, or types.

I have been sitting for an hour or so at a desk in my monastic cell, tasting the dark morning hours. During this time, I have sensed each of these modes. First, there were the dim moon shadows, bathing the landscape in mystery. The luminous darkness emitted a tangible silence. I felt drawn to it, toward a primal peace, a unity without parts—warm, welcoming, belonging, grounded.

I have no idea how long it was before I became aware of a row of cottonwoods, marking the monastic lane in the first hints of dawn. I saw just enough to sense a pattern—from the trees to the rise and fall of the mountain range, passing out of sight in the mist. It evoked remembrance of other mornings, when the same feeling was evoked by the pattern of fence posts, or ordered bales of hay, stretching out of sight. Exact. Precise. Formed. Things as they are "intended" to be. Order. Always.

Not long ago the sun arose, filtering through the fall aspens. I was lured outside, as if to be officially greeted. It would have been a sin to remain still. The dance began slowly, tentatively, as the sleepy murmurings of birds mounted toward a persistent din. I had forgotten how much each morning is a birthing, a variation on the theme of becoming. Lilting. Ecstatic. Movement. Awaking.

All three modes, within an hour. It was almost too quick—and too much.

In transition from God's triune functionings, from Creator to Redeemer, it is wise to refer back to the understanding of Trinity from which spiritual pluralism emerges. The first three spirit types we have described reflect the Trinity of Essence. To be invaded by the Abyss, to be shaped graciously by Logos, to be swept and impelled by Spirit—these three point profoundly toward the interiority of God. Together they express our experience of the One in whom we live (type 1), and move (type 3), and have our being (type 2). Such encounters are self-justifying, valued for their own sake, intrinsically nurturing. To ask, "What good do they do?" is not to have had the experience, or at least to have missed the meaning. And as marks of Presence, imaging God as God is in God's self, they also forge a sensitivity to ourselves as created in that triune image. Therefore, to experience the reverse side of these spirit types is to be discovered by hints of what it means to be truly ourselves.

In turning now to the remaining spirit types, we move in the direction of the Trinity of Manifestation—as expressive of God's activity in the world. Thus a diagonal arrow on our diagram expresses the Divine movement from the Abyss as Mystery (type 1) to the final Vision as the Cocreative call to Creativity (type 9). The overarching movement is from Nothingness to the fullness of Being. Once one understands the whole, each of the nine types can be experienced from either of the two perspectives we have used to understand the Trinity—as essence or as manifestation.

In experiencing any of these types in terms of "essence," one is drawn to lose oneself in that particular mode of God. Through the use of discipline, the experience can become increasingly divorced from content and particularity, becoming valued for its own sake. Each mode becomes, in its own way, a permission to *be*. Such experiences are contemplative, direct, and unmeditated, as we saw in describing the loss of self in abyss, logos, and becoming. This perspective is most natural for introverts, whose rich interiority is disposed to sense the essential as Within.

Within such experiences, however, is a creative tension between the actual and the possible, the real and the dream. Thus each type becomes in its own way a call to *do*. Such experiences are less for their own sake, then, and more mediated and inferential. It is as though one is invited to place a wager on a promising metaphor, thereby practicing its implicit meaning into believability through commitment. Here one does not participate in God as much as in a cosmos whose mystery, order, and dynamism are rumors and innuendoes of the Divine. Such spirituality is most natural for extroverts, whose penchant for objects, events, and people brings a preference for spiritual types that are wedded outwardly—enfleshed and passionate.

While each person needs to develop both "essential" and "manifest" orientations into a holistic spirituality, one of these orientations needs to be recognized as most promising for maturation as one's spiritual home base. Once claimed, the direction for one's spiritual pilgrimage is determined—to move toward the edges of the most unfamiliar.

In describing these first three spiritual types, then, we have experienced the meanings characteristic of the "Essential Trinity."

Yet we have gained, as well, experiential hints concerning the "Manifest Trinity." The direction in which the next chapters will move is increasingly from God's nature into God's doing—as God's mysterious richness flows out upon the vast cosmos as God's magnum opus.

6

Fragility and the Gift of Life

Type 4: Contingency

In the spirit types to which we now turn, spirituality will become less a solitary discipline and more a style related to the texture of active life. Exterior reality becomes increasingly the arena by which to focus metaphorically the Divine activity.

The fourth spirit type is evoked by one cryptic word—dangling. In the first type, we explored the meaning of the Christian insistence that God created everything from nothing. There we focused positively on the experience that results, in which everything is grounded in mystery. Within the fourth type, this condition, identified as dependency, is viewed from its underbelly, as the state of contingency. The first spirit type often requires a prior encounter with this fourth one. Such an encounter can come through the specter of death, in any of its many forms of fact or possibility. Thus this spirit type does not stray far from one fact: that no amount of anxiety can add one cubit to the span of one's life.

Fragility and Giftness

Every finite relationship has some degree of freedom in which to say, "No thanks." But there is one relationship in which we have no freedom, none whatsoever. In the face of death, the only option is no option but to say yes to the "No." I can in no way negate death when it comes. It simply *is*, absolutely so, on its own terms, as naked fact.

Yet this recognition can bring a transforming illumination. What is true at the moment of death is simply an acting out of what is true of every instant of life. I do not exist because I make it happen. *How* I exist, at least in part, is mine to say. But the fact *that* I exist, in this moment or any moment, has nothing to do with me. I can end life, but I cannot cause it to be. Therefore, to be created does not mean that now I exist on some sort of permanent basis. I have no choice but to exist on the dole, one second at a time. And what is true of me is true of every speck of the universe, and the universe as a whole. Each and every fragment is created, moment by moment, gift by gift, with no strength of sustenance within itself whatsoever. If God should forget any part, it would no longer be.

Spirit types 1 and 4, then, focus on contrasting ends of this primal relation constituting life. In type 1, one participates in the pregnant Abyss from which all things flow, continually. From it springs the yearning to be lost in a nurturing return to that primal womb. Its most graphic expression is the mystic moment, an eternal now, in which all distinctions merge in reunion. Life into death, death into life—the cycle of death and rebirth, as an organic and spiritual Whole.

In this fourth type, however, the focus is on the "feel" of that which *does* exist, experiencing itself as constituted through separation from its Ground. Here one experiences the self as dangling, as orphan, as exile, over the Abyss of nothingness. And while in type 7 this dimension can open up into a delicious, lyric freedom of self-abandonment, here the feeling of existing is one of ontic *fragility*.

The philosopher Berkeley was fascinated by the fact that a stone that he observed one day *continued* to exist the next morning. Type 1 is fascinated with the mystery that anything exists at all. Type 4 marvels at its continuity—the endurance of anything that *does* exist. One becomes intrigued by the conditional, the accidental, the incidental—the self-contradictory nature of the fact that anything *remains in existence*. Given this contingent feel of everything, the primal experience of this spirit type is that of being *sustained*, ongoingly. The sheer fact of my living is an illusion unless I am being held in being by One who is Self-caused. Finite existence is an ongoing surd, possible only in being repeatedly given, instant by instant.

Absurdity as Redemption

Tillich was so impressed by this experience that he centered his understanding of redemption on it. Any claim to have a right to existence is about as absurd as sending a light bulb to an undeveloped nation, assuming that it will glow because these people have a right to light. Work as hard as we might, up to our final breath, none of us will ever be able to justify this statement: "I deserve to exist." Yet we workaholics try—do we ever! That is the absurdity with which this spirit type converges with the offer of redemption.

When the reality of one's radical contingency dawns, perhaps on a vulnerable birthday, or the death of someone disturbingly close, then the real absurdity appears. Negatively, absurdity rests in the loss. But there is a strangely positive side—that there is anything to lose. I continue to exist although I have no more reason for doing so than any of the countless lives being snuffed out daily. Thus, simply to continue existing, I myself or anything, for even a moment, is incredible gift—the pearl of great price, given and regiven, momentary gift beside momentary gift, donation, loan, pittance, allotment, allowance, portion.

Here one becomes enmeshed in one fatal and transforming fact. Those who seek to lay claim to their life, to gain control of it, to own it as their own right, who consume themselves with work in an effort to justify their right to be alive—these are the ones who will lose their life, having existed without ever having lived. Blessed are those who give up trying, for they are the ones who will find their lives, as a gift coat of many colors. Therefore, to gain is to lose; but to lose is to gain (Matt. 10:39). To so live life is to be "graced." But the grace evaporates as manna the instant one takes one's life or possessions for granted, or claims them either as possessions or as deserved. Grace is never grace unless it is experienced as a "nevertheless."

The Boundary

In a real sense, the primal experience we are describing is one that every person craves to have—*to feel accepted, unconditionally, in spite of one's unacceptability*.[1] Yet the incredible irony is this: we are not open to hearing that good news—that before we did anything, our lives were already gifts to be accepted, given at one's first moment as if an "infant baptism." Instead, our overwhelming temptation is to disguise our contingency in shame, covering our vulnerability with assorted fig leaves, refusing to walk naturally in the cool of the day (Gen. 3:4–11). "Codependency," the current popular accounting for an unhealthy psyche, could render all dependency a cause for shame. The rebellious Adam is being resurrected as cult hero—the self-made person, needing no one, cool, aloof, utterly autonomous, with every needed power as close as one's back pocket.

Thus we are socialized to hide that very state without which unconditional acceptance is impossible. Actually, the situation is worse. We attempt to hide through the bravado of power—white over black, Protestant over Catholic, rich over poor. "The things we do called sins are nothing but manifestations of our desire to show ourselves and others that we are worthy of being loved."[2] Yet the more we try to prove our worth, the more unlovable we become, unless the vicious circle is cracked. And this crack, going through every foundation, has a name—contingency.

The role of the Hebrew prophets is well understood from this perspective. When Israel was fragile, insecure, dependent, and in need, the people fervently called on God; but when they became plump, prosperous, and arrogant, they no longer relied on God but made application themselves for the job. Idolatry is the prophets' name for any situation in which this spirit mode is permitted to fall into disrepute. Without it, there is no such thing as a teachable spirit.

The human tendency is not simply to disregard the prophets, but to quiet them, one way or the other. This clarifies, in part, the role of the Jew as scapegoat of history. Rather than hear the call involved in this spirit mode, we prefer to persecute the caller.

> The existence of the Jew reveals something which is otherwise concealed—that no one, neither people nor individual, really has a home in world history, that no one is finally secure, that we are all pushed about, that we are all eternal strangers, since it is only in God that we are finally at home and secure.[3]

Herein rests the indispensability of the spirit type we are exploring. We humans have an ongoing need to have our pride punctured—by exposure to the fundamental fact that we *dangle* for our existence, on a short thread. "Fool! This night your soul is required of you" (Luke 12:20). Ontic shock. This spirit type is imperative, then, for all of us—for those who lead the parade and for those of us who lose ourselves in the crowd along the parade route. It is the mode that never permits us to stray far from life on the boundary.

The Denial of Death

Writer Henry Miller, hardly known for being religious, nevertheless sensed this basic condition. Looking down from an elevated train, one of his characters mumbled, "Everywhere, death,

death." Transfixed by the dirty ice in the gutter where a dead cat lay, he knew that for the first time he had looked at death and grasped it. From that moment on, "I knew what it was to be isolated."

Some historians have suggested that earlier periods of history were more religious than ours because of the short life span people experienced. Even within Puritan America, the odds were against surviving birth. In contrast, "total care" is the code word in modern America for regarding life as a right, with the option to be frozen for later recall. Yet, in spite of ourselves, the shadow of nuclear contingency is giving rebirth to this spirit mode for some. One stubby finger on a small red button is a very short thread. Paul insisted that this condition was universal for Christians:

> "we are being killed all the day long;
> we are regarded as sheep to be slaughtered."
> (Rom. 8:36)

While several spirit modes spin off from this primal relation, it is the task of type 4 to keep a sustained focus on our *ongoing fragility*. Life is enigma—ominously and redemptively. The shadow that falls over the whole is an ultimate fact: that what is given in each moment can just as quickly be taken away in any moment. But the meaning behind the shadow, making the desert bloom, is that while all indeed will be taken away, to be bitten by this awareness is to have *today* rendered into a precious gift of tender grace. Take no thought of the morrow, not because, as in Ecclesiastes, it will simply be a tedious repetition of today, and of yesterday. Rather, if one lives each day as if it were the last, then there can never be a day quite like this one.

EXERCISES

1. *The Desert Experience*

There is a resurgence of interest in the spirituality of the early desert mothers and fathers. This is probably a reaction to our present starvation by affluence. Without fasting, a daily Thanksgiving is only fattening. Without a Good Friday, Easter is an exercise in hyperbole. Therefore spirituality formed by this mode resides in full recognition of life as having not only highs but lows, not only the full but the empty, not only a presence but an absence. The name for this spiritual experience is the desert. It is essential, especially in today's culture of invasive togetherness where all secrets of the heart are viewed as subject to a parental or marriage right to know. Simple sanity requires time alone, and wisdom of any depth is impossible without the solitude of the wilderness.

This desert experience is hard to understand, let alone acquire, in a culture of affluence such as ours, fueled by the cult of self-gratification. Thus we need to describe it in some detail. The desert calls for an exercise in faith alone. It occurs wherever one is thrust into a barrenness that offers little support. There God's presence is known primarily as an absence, where acknowledged fallibility, poverty, and incompetence are confessed in color on the newsprint of one's mind. This mode involves choosing marginality, at least for a time, as life's most honest posture.

David Knight is helpful in pondering why there is such an interest today in monasticism, while so few persons are willing to become committed monks. The enthusiasts are interested in the "call of the mountains"—seeking something better, probably "a healthier human existence" and a "supportive community of deeper personal relationships." The key for them is experience, for the mountains are not where one stays. One receives something there, and then leaves. This is the spirituality of the positive way. The negative version, by contrast, entails a rejection of both gratification and fulfillment. It entails a turning point where one knows that "one is no longer free to turn back with fidelity."[4] Actually the desert is any place in which simply to survive is a triumph. There one lives the truth that faith at its naked heart is a commitment to see things through, no matter what. This makes life itself a spirit quest.

Abraham and Sarah are models, called as they were to leave the Fertile Crescent for desert places unknown. "Saddle up, we're moving out." "Where are we going?" "I'll tell you when we get there." And they went, marching off the map of what they knew as the civilized world.

In our time, entering the desert may mean having or choosing a minority status—drinking life at the margins, and stepping to a drummer whose beat is without society's imprimatur. It entails at least a symbolic refusal to air-condition the hot, or heat the cold, or light the dark, or shade the light. It means stretching oneself to the edge, without the padded comfort of an exercise machine.

From the vantage of this mode, the humble invisibility of Jesus comes into relief. His was a hidden life for thirty years. And when he did appear, without press agent, this simple carpenter went even deeper into this spirit mode, with forty days and forty nights in the literal desert. Even during the year or two he had left to live, he drew away periodically from the hurting crowds into the solace of lonely places. Going, "as was his custom," to the final abandonment of a garden vigil, he was crucified with criminals as the condemned one, disgraced in nakedness on a dung heap outside the city gate. And we? "Whoever would be followers of mine, let them renounce themselves and take up their crosses" (Matt. 16:24, author's translation). This is the desert call.

It involves, at its deepest level, that near physical pain of loneliness which points to Jesus' and our final ache of heart. For some, the name for the desert may be a psychiatrist's office. These, it has been said, may be the ones with integrity, for they have difficulty accommodating to hollow respectability. In the desert, symbolic or literal, one can learn the kind of dependence Jesus celebrated as belonging to the child. It is where, with Job, one girds one's loins and faces the silence of God. The Trappist Charles Cummings distills this spiritual depth in a sentence: it requires that "sometime, somewhere, everything needs to be up for grabs." The desert, then, is an exercise in self-emptying and self-surrender. "In the desert we go on serving the God whom we do not see, loving [the God] whom we do not feel, adoring [the God] whom we do not understand, and thanking [the God] who has taken from us everything but [God's self]."[5]

All of us have endured periods of depression, at least the edges of burnout, and the vulnerability of sickness. Usually we experience such times on the physical or psychological levels. But these are invitations into the desert, not only to the place where this spirit mode can be forged, but to where one can find an index of one's spiritual depth. There are few saints who have not known such purgings, usually for an extended time. They testify, at this basic level of desert spirituality, that faith, in the end, cannot be based on the sands of *any* experience. Faith means perseverance in practice, as expression of a preposterous truth in God—"for better, for worse, for richer, for poorer, in sickness and in health . . ." Oh, yes, "until we are parted by death."

Each of us needs a sacred alone place in which to let the desert experience occur. For some it is an actual hermitage, constructed for precisely this purpose. This was Thoreau's reason for building his shack on Walden Pond: "To drive life into a corner, and reduce it to its lowest terms." Why? Because "I wished to live deliberately, to front only the essential facts of life, and see if I could not learn what it had to teach, and not, when I came to die, discover that I had not lived."[6] There are times when life must be stripped to its essentials. "Take nothing for your journey" (Luke 9:3).

The desert experience is easy to arrange; the difficulty is in enduring it. The primal requirement is going where one will be alone for a period of time sufficient to stretch one's certainty as to the ability to do it. Arm yourself only with minimal "essentials," plus paper and pencil. If one has never seen a literal hermitage, imagine one's ancestors in a solitary two-room farmhouse somewhere on the Great Plains. Or remember driving alone in the dark on unfamiliar roads.

A hermitage can be a day or afternoon each month in a place (even a room or a corner of one's house) that is designated as holy space. Furnish it as a place for stillness, away from all duties, into which one takes only one's self. It means resisting the temptation to flee that place for the sake of "productive work." The healing comes in remaining where being alone and doing nothing are sufficient. The goal is to establish the "hermitage of the heart."[7] There is particular solace in such a state if one prays for a sense of mutuality with all the lonely persons over the face of the earth, making one's ache a common call.

Whatever form one's exercises in this spirit mode may take, the discipline of the desert is particularly mandatory for those of us who are the "driven" ones. We are the ones who hide our spiritual insecurities by taking pride in not taking a day off, or forfeiting vacations out of a sense of "duty," or boasting in having our calendars in place for the next year, or even two.

"Outward Bound" is an educational experiment that provides geographic contexts that push individuals beyond what they think to be their limits. Each of us probably knows privately what such a testing would be for oneself. Once, for me, it entailed a pilgrimage of hiking down and up the Grand Canyon in one day. The popularity of health clubs may reflect an unconscious suspicion that flabbiness of body is somehow related to sloppiness of spirit. If so, how ironic is the ad: "Our machines make it possible to exercise without fatigue." Thus an important spiritual exercise in this mode would be to design one's own "outward bound." You alone know what you are most inclined to avoid because it is most needed.

For some, the most immediate path into the desert is marked "diet." Few enter it spiritually. To do so entails recognizing it as a variation on the discipline of "fasting." Here desert "failure" becomes identified as variation on the theme of perseverance. Unfortunately, much of the booming business in diet products and gimmicks is an effort to despiritualize this opportunity. The offer, with "money-back guarantee," is a scheme to benefit from the desert experience through economic rather than spiritual cost. The ads might well read, " 'Desert' as 'Dessert.' " I know well the temptation—to sip a cocktail in the restaurant on the rim of the Grand Canyon, and watch.

There is reason to believe that without a literal wilderness, humankind withers. To tame the last frontier is to turn the eagle into a tame pigeon begging for popcorn. In many states, there are wilderness areas inviting one into the desert experience. The rule is a spiritual principle: restrict conveniences to those which you can carry on your back.

Several years ago, I proposed that each seminary student go on a solitary retreat for half a day. In anger, the professor of pastoral care and counseling declared that I would be personally responsible for any psychic disorders that might occur. If his uneasiness has truth, the desert is no further away than scheduling time alone with one's self, without diversion. One may have tasted the beginnings of this experience in a hospital waiting room after you have read all the magazines. What is most humbling and threatening about the desert experience is having to live self-consciously with one's self as roommate.[8]

2. Ascetic Practices

A rhythm of self-chosen deprivation has long been important to spirit life. Christmas has its Advent, and Easter its Lent. Fasting has been an important practice within this rhythm. In the Methodist tradition, in fact, each member of the clergy, by ordination vow, is required both to practice and to teach fasting. This discipline is particularly powerful when coupled with events fraught with theological significance.

A full fast means to be physically nurtured only by liquid, or perhaps by bread and water. In most monasteries, this occurs on Ash Wednesday and Good Friday. In addition, on Ash Wednesday one's forehead is marked with ashes, with the words, "From dust you have come, and to dust you will return" are said. The Good Friday equivalent is to approach with bare feet the crucifix, kissing the nail in the feet of Jesus. This is one's response to having heard the words, "My God, my God, why hast thou forsaken me?

. . . And Jesus cried again with a loud voice and yielded up his spirit" (Matt. 27:46, 50). A partial fast, such as refraining from meat, has been a way of sanctifying each Friday as a Good Friday.

Unfortunately today, even in Roman Catholic churches, there is a tendency to eliminate such ascetic practices, with even Lenten sacrifice viewed as morbid, body-denying, and negative. While such practices can and have been overdone, the spiritual truth is that without denial the will grows flabby, character becomes confused with personality, joy is reduced to trivial cheerfulness, and self-gratification thrives as individualism.

I still lend to special people a cherished book I once wanted so badly that I went without eating in order to buy it. For some of us, fasting might well be to refrain from hurry, taking on no new commitments until the priorities become resifted. Others find it important to fast one day each week, sometimes by sharing with other fasters a meal of bread and water. The money saved is given to those whose deprivation is not voluntary.

Bonhoeffer once said that when Christ calls, he bids one come and die. T. S. Eliot confessed the consequence—that the world should hate the church, for it reminds all of us of what none of us want to hear. "I will show you fear in a handful of dust."[9] Martin Heidegger claimed that what defines one's whole life is how one dies one's death.

Helpful exercises to see one's life from the perspective of one's end are these:

- Compose your own funeral service.
- Write, and periodically read, your will—as a liturgy.
- Do a meditation on the subject "If I had two months to live." Then try "If I had four hours to live." Let your imagination flow, over the where, how, why, with whom, and so what.
- We are told that newspapers are obsessed with accidents, violence, and death. Read one edition from just that perspective. It is amazing how few persons seem to die at the "end" of their life.
- Imagine yourself in a casket in a funeral parlor, then in the ground. Write about your feelings.

3. *Liturgy of the Hours*

From early times, the church has divided the twenty-four-hour day by the Trinity, rendering eight three-hour segments in which to practice daily the inclusive rhythm of Christian life. The eight offices (liturgies), still preserved in many monasteries, are readily available for use by others. A shortened version appears in *Christian Prayer: The Liturgy of the Hours.*[10] Particularly important for the spirit mode we are exploring are the times of Vigils, marking the day's beginning, and Compline, as its completion.

For monks, the dark hours of Vigils are most sacred, with Trappists rising around 3 A.M. These hours form the visual and aural time for experiencing contingency. As you remember, we met at the kitchen table, as the city slept. In the inner city, it is the time not to go out alone. In rural areas, Vigils are accompanied by the summer sound of coyotes and the winter howling of night winds. The comparable biblical parable is that of the virgins waiting with lamps lighted. These are the hours when most persons die, for it is when our hold on life is by its thinnest thread. These are the hours when it is too late to sleep, too early to do. Together they symbolize the in-between time, the feel of Holy Saturday, the patient posture of condemned waiting. These are the hours when illusions are few, for in looking "in a mirror dimly," the seeing "face to face" is most often a reflection of one's own (1 Cor. 13:12).

Compline is the final act of one's day. It means "complete." It is the time for making peace with the world, and thus with God. In preparation, one does whatever one would need to do if this were one's final night. To whom should one telephone, write, or speak —what confessions, what regrets, what forgiveness, what thankfulness yet unoffered? It ends with the words, "And now may the all-powerful Lord grant us a restful night and a peaceful death." One is sprinkled with water, recalling one's baptism as having been into Christ's death and resurrection. Thereby wrapped in the hope that one's death has already been died, one relinquishes one's hold on life, and enters "the great Silence." Life is given only one day at a time, and that day is now over. "Into your hands I commend my spirit." If I should have another day, it will be sheer gift. Thus without Compline, Lauds as the daybreak celebration of resurrection is empty.

As a minimal exercise, rise early enough to taste the dark before the dawn. Simply get in touch with the feel of that time, nothing more. For a second exercise, choose a special evening in which to make a list of what would need to be done if this were your final Compline. Do as many of these things as you can do. Then let go, probably in a way that you have not been able to do before. Monks sleep very well.

Using traditional liturgies for each of these hours, or improvising one's own, can be an important exercise in exploring daily the spirit life as pluralistic.

4. *Meditate*

One's list of words for focused meditation here might include: arbitrary, dangling, fragile, ominous, desert, contingent, boundary, finitude, dependence, tentativeness, enigma, strangeness, exile, adrift, discontinuity, opaque, inscrutable, night, alone, death.

5. *Music*

The sound that quietly holds together this mode can be heard well in Barber's Adagio for Strings. Other possibilities include Fauré's *Requiem,* Victoria's *Requiem,* Bach's "Come Sweet Death," and, from Mahler, his Symphony No. 4 (third movement), Symphony No. 5 (fourth movement), and Symphony No. 10 (Adagio). These are sober sounds of perseverance, of melancholy determination, of integrity forged by endurance. It is a quality that infects the varied voices of Carole King, Janis Joplin, Roberta Flack, and Rita Coolidge. In jazz, it is the sound of the "blues," that sweet impossibility that renders the anguish of simple endurance a moral victory. It is what can make the return from the cemetery, in the idiom of black jazz, an enigmatic jamming of joy.

6. *Painting*

Useful in focusing this spirit type is Grunëwald's famous crucifixion from the Isenheim Altarpiece.[11] Stripped of all delicateness, the ambience is one of heavy paradox. The greenish horror of death's greedy malevolence is bathed in an impossible promise by the pointing finger of the disciple John. The "man of sorrows" is very God of very God. Here is the unbelievable enigma, that humanity, claimed by its final contingency, is at that very moment a disclosure of the Divine. Such awareness is not by sight, but by faith as wager. The paradox etching even the edges of terror is fashioned with conjunctions: however, yet, notwithstanding, although—and "be that as it may."

A Summary

Nothing is of itself, and thus of itself is as the grass that withers. Each fading flower is a foreboding hint that one's nature is nothingness. The focus is not on the certainty of one's eventual demise, but on the uncanny strangeness of existing *now*. Without apparent cause, I am. The fact that I, as a "no," nevertheless continue to exist is a deep "yes." Amazing is the serious authenticity that comes by facing without flinching the insufficiency of one's widowed state. Here the courage to be is birthed—by that about life which one neither wants nor can willingly relinquish. Hope is the simple trust that God has not forgotten the recipe for manna.

Contingency as spirit life is the act of giving away our nothingness. It is a mode broad enough to link an Ignatius of Loyola and a John Wesley. Ignatius prays,

> Take all my freedom, my memory, my understanding, and my will. All that I have and cherish you have given me. I surrender it all . . . your grace and your love are wealth enough for me. . . . I ask for nothing more.[12]

And from the Watchnight liturgy, Wesley prays to

> be no longer mine but yours. . . . Put me to doing, put me to suffering; let me be employed for you or laid aside for you, exalted for you or brought low for you. Let me be full, let me be empty. Let me have all things, let me have nothing. I freely and heartily yield all things to your pleasure and disposal.[13]

While type 1 focuses on creation, type 4 focuses on redemption. To awaken to the miracle of continuity is to be reconciled with the Redeemer as Sustainer, in such a way that "now but not yet" becomes good news. Therein the provisional becomes a "proviso," whereby one can live life as a tenuous and tender gift, one day, one hour, one moment at a time. Alcoholics Anonymous may need to lead the way.

7

Companionship
and the Divine
Guest Appearance

Type 5: Incarnation

The Christian claim is that with this fifth spirit mode the other spiritual dimensions converge with revealing uniqueness. And it, in turn, becomes the prism through which the other modes are clarified, enriched, affirmed, and validated. Here *the* Incarnation becomes the disclosure of incarnation as the grounding heart of all reality. The God who has no need of creation has willed not to be God without us, covenanting with the cosmos to be the place of God's own dwelling. Therefore the Incarnation is our personal invitation to be cocreators with God—not only in midwifing the creation, but in tasting even now the transfiguration yet to be. The cosmos is in God, for God is in the world. Such a disclosure, for the Christian, is very concrete, having a human face and a Jewish name.

Thus the gospel hinges on a historic event, for its good news is the revelation of God as Companion Friend—in, with, and for creation. Jesus as the Christ is the pledge in flesh and blood that authenticates the fullness of pluralistic spirituality. Commitment at this one point justifies our gambling regarding the other spirit modes, that they are in fact intonations of the really real. What is involved at this central point is not a story about God. Rather, God tells God's own story, acting it out as a play within the play.

Trusting the Experience

In chanting Psalm 88 at Vespers one night, the need for this central mode became graphic. One sentence struck me:

> "Friend and neighbor you have taken away:
> my one companion is darkness"
> (Ps. 87:18, Paulist [Hebrew, 88:18]).

Each of us has had at least a few of the experiences we are developing as spirit types. But *can they be trusted?* Are they in truth the finite underbelly of a Triune Reality justifying the surname God? Or, in the end, are they only respites from the midnight anxiety, so that, in the end, our only companion *is* darkness?

A recognition disclosed in the desert experience becomes a conclusion here. In the end, all we have are experiences whose interpretation is unverifiable, and thus the meanings of which have only the certainty of a gamble. Life *is* faith. Even if one wagers one's life on ultimate meaninglessness, that is no less a gamble. Interesting is the response of the famed atheist A. J. Ayers to a recent brush with death. Having had what he acknowledged as an out-of-body experience, he stated: "It simply makes my gamble that there is nothing beyond death a bit less certain." And so it is for the Christian, working the other side of the street. The risk entailed in declaring these spirit modes to be valid focuses on one question: "But who do you say that I am?" (Matt. 16:15).

Prayer as Expressed Friendship

This makes prayer, in the etymological sense, the central discipline for this spirit type. Prayer means "to ask," or, more broadly, "to dialogue" or "to babble," as with a friend. This mode involves spirituality as intimacy of relationship. Thus, just as communication is at the heart of human relationships, so prayer is essential to the Divine-human one. This is so much so that Joachim Jeremias claims that the uniqueness of Christianity centers in the first two words of the Lord's Prayer: "Our Abba." The best translation of this unique name Jesus had for God is Daddy/Mommy.[1]

Unbelievably, Jesus' use of that word is the declaration that the God of all space and time, the Fecundity of formed and restless Being, the One so inexhaustible in complexity and sweep as to shatter all imagination, the God who can cup the waters of the seas in the palm of one hand, this very One *wills to be our intimate companion, closer even than we are to ourselves.* God's autobiography as the Jesus-story has as its punch line God's trusting us with God's own name—Emmanuel, "God with us." With God as the surname and Emmanuel the given name, we meet the One eager to enter every finitude, every carnal and earthy part of ourselves and our world, inviting intimacy on a first-name basis. This God of Unfathomable Mystery, of Staggering Order, of Sweeping Power—this is the One who here comes as a Shepherdess, cuddling the lambs to her bosom.

The Promise

Prayer as "companion dialogue," then, is our way of acting out the story of the Divine Guest Appearance, a drama whose unbelievability resides in its being too good to be true. God has *chosen intimacy*, thereby declaring that the Divine-human relation, in all its rich pluralism, is at heart a love affair. "I have called you by name, you are mine" (Isa. 42:1, author's translation). To us who live in the shadow of death, this God promises in blood: "I will not forget you. Behold, I have graven you on the palms of my hands" (Isa. 49:15–16). This engraving has been done with nails.

Relationships often stumble over the fear that "if you really knew me, you wouldn't like me." So our relations remain, at least in part, a game called "Pretense," with no other option in sight. But what if God so shares our finitude as to know us better than we know ourselves, and *still* accepts us? Amazing, for such a relationship would be unlike every other relationship that we have ever had, or can have. Once you know that God knows everything about you, you are free.

The Mutual Test

We can begin to see the grounding that is necessary if the amazing contention entailed by this mode is to be true. The test of any relation is whether one is able to argue, talk back, find fault, display anger and hurt with full confidence that nothing can impair that relation. The foundation for such confidence concerning the Divine-human relationship has a name and a place, and thus it becomes the intersection marking the center point of history. The place is Golgotha, epitomizing all that we could do to "test" the Divine-human relationship—betrayal, scourging, lies, spitting, blood, murder. And the response? Resurrection is the declaration that the relation is still in place, firmly and eternally so.

If this is so, then the "companion darkness" characterizing our time receives amazing illumination. It is an emptiness craving for Incarnation, an absence yearning for Presence, because it is a restlessness being lured forth by the One in whose triune image we have been fashioned. Thus the midnight restlessness, after all, is not the sour residue marking atheism's modern inevitability. It is a restlessness forging the centerpiece of our hope and our spirituality, for us and for history. The birth of God in each self, and the resurrection of each self into God—this is the plot called history. It is what calls us into storytelling as a way of living.

Life as Covenant

The first three spirit modes were variations on the theme of self-loss: into mystery, into order, and into dynamism. But in this spirit type, instead of being drawn into Otherness, the Other enters and declares God's self to be at home within us. Unlike the first three, however, the focus is not on unity, but on relationship. In that difference, the centrality of this mode becomes evident. *Relationship is essential to the very constitution and completion of Reality.* Thus the basic unit of reality is not God. Nor is it humans. It is God *and* humanity, together, in relationship. God has willed it to be, gloriously so.

Thus, no matter how disruptive and perverted we become, life at its heart is good, because each speck of life is the friend of God. And while absorption and self-negation into God are important parts of Christian spirituality, to see these as the *heart* of spirituality is to undermine the center of Christianity. God's assumption of humanness is the Divine wedding with creation, in a relationship of intimacy beyond the point of recall. Reality will never be as if we never were. Eternally.

Being and Doing

At this point, the classic distinction between monastic and apostolic spiritualities makes sense. The first three types we have explored tend to be monastic—a forfeiture of self for the sake of "pure" experience. Each is a disciplined and withdrawn solitariness, centering in absorbing silence. Apostolic or "diffused" spirituality, on the other hand, draws one into the daily doing of one's calling ("apostolate"). Unfortunately, these distinctions of "being" and "doing" have often been viewed as warring alternatives. It is in type 5 that both can be seen in their necessary intersection. Drawing analogies from human relationships, it is apparent how indispensable is the eager dialogue of companions, never having enough time to share all that they have been doing. But equally important is the fireside quietness of lovers, those times together "after all these years" in which silence expresses best the union that has been the grounding assumption throughout. So with God.

Here and Now

T. S. Eliot sees spirit life as beginning with hints of incarnation, followed by guesses, whose validation is Incarnation. For most of us, there are only the occasional "unattended Moments," such as losing oneself in music or in the smell of wild thyme. Thus our need, he insists, is for discipline rooted by faith in this central mode. By wagering on *the* Incarnation, one can increasingly discern as valid the "intersection of the timeless with time"—in each moment, in every crevice, at life's binding edges.[2]

Thus as Incarnation becomes a way of life, one is moved to enter the spirit modes that we will soon explore under the rubric of God's activity as Sanctifier. Emmanuel, "God with us," gives grounding for the eyes of promise (type 7), of sacramental presence (type 8), and of vision (type 9). This is a way of saying that the reverse face of *God seeing with us*, is our *seeing with God*.

In this fifth mode, however, attention is drawn away from both past and future. The center is here and now, as the *present of the Presence*—where life as the relationship of ceaseless prayer has its excitement.

EXERCISES

1. *Practicing the Presence*

Brother Lawrence expresses with awesome simplicity one way in which this spirit mode can be disciplined—as "practice of the presence." The "how" comes in treating God as one would one's closest companion. As a cook for years in a monastery, Lawrence found it natural to share with God the smell of the soup he made. He surmised that his Divine Friend found delight as well in the crack of crisp carrots, the interior star of a cut apple, the smell of fresh herbs. Presence, he insists, is the practice of sharing—in, with, and through everything that is, hinting of the world as kitchen hearth. His daily prayer is simple: "I beg thee to grant me the grace to remain with thee and to keep thee company; but that it may be the better done, my Lord, work with me, receive my labors and possess all my affection."[3]

Thus while the mystic tendencies characterizing the first three modes are rooted in the Essential Trinity, Brother Lawrence reveals in type 5 the heart of the Trinity of Manifestation. The "mystic" God in light inexpressible wills to "keep company" in the earth garden. Here, in the cool of the day, God's Being and God's Doing commingle, as "contemplation" becomes "diffused" into the daily conversations of eager companions. In this mode, instead of inviting us to go apart, God asks to walk with us. We are discovered, then, by the God who has chosen to call earth home, in all its width and breadth and depth and height.

Act as a friend. Would I invite a friend into my home, Brother Lawrence asks, and then forget she or he was there, or give that friend the silent treatment? The exercise suggested here is one of applying daily to one's relationship with God precisely the treatment one already knows to be appropriate for a friend or lover. Conversation, gifts, quiet enjoyment, shared meals by candlelight, walks to favorite places, hard work together. The difficulty is not in learning *how* to do it, but in *remembering* to do it. It requires intentional discipline to break a lifetime lived on the working assumption that one is fundamentally alone. Thus, transition from singleness to a Divine-human married life will be as difficult as it is rewarding.

You may initially feel self-conscious doing this next exercise, so set aside a short but different time for practice each day. Live that part of the day exactly as you ordinarily would, but with one addition. Act as if there is with you a friend who has never been in your city before. Upon arriving, the friends ask, "What are you going to do today?" Then give Jesus' reply: "Come and see." Treat such periods as rehearsals, with the goal being a habitual disposition to live your whole life relationally.

Use vocatives. Evelyn Underhill once suggested that a person give up the practice of long prayers for a while. Instead, use "darts of prayer," one-liners, as it were, thrown to God. These could be like the "sweet nothings" that make falling in love so special. Indicative of such a relation is the emergence of nicknames—special, often secret names of endearment. One might ponder what God's pet name for you might be.

Interestingly, Israel's way of exercising this special relationship was through a totally opposite practice. In recognizing the power of a name, its people refused the presumption of calling God by name. Instead, to bury that name in the silence of one's heart was to honor the specialness of the fact that "God" had trusted Israel with that proper name, "Jehovah" or "Yahweh." A name is important. Moses asked for God's true name: "Who shall I say sent me?" "I am who I am," was God's wary response. But in Jesus, God whispered the name as a guest appearance—"Emmanuel." The only image for God that I need, said my hermit friend, is the name Jesus. Perhaps even better is "Jeshua," the precise sound of the name Mary and Joseph used for him. Humans, and presumably God, enjoy being called by name.

2. Consciousness as Dialogical

Consciousness is the process by which the self becomes aware of itself. It is acted out as an incessant chatter of "I" with "me." So deeply habitual is this practice that often we find ourselves talking to ourselves aloud, and in our sleep. Contemplation, or the "prayer of centering," as described in type 1, has as its goal a halting of this chattering. The exercise we propose here is the opposite. The goal is to transform our babbling into prayer. This is done by rendering this constant self-dialogue, which is as natural as life itself, into an ongoing Divine-human conversation.

As a beginning, intersperse a name for God into the midst of your ordinary babbling. "God, why on earth is he making a fool of himself?" Or "Jeshua, I'm feeling terribly lonely, and I don't know what to do." By turning babble into address, expressions of puzzlement and lament become transformed into expressions of relationship in a companionship of mutual support and struggle. Once again, how to do this exercise is simple; remembering to do it, and therefore to break a lifetime pattern, is another matter.

Bonhoeffer is helpful in understanding the fuller implications of such an exercise. In becoming a Christian, he insists, one can never again see anything nakedly. Having the "mind of Christ" means having Christ as mediator, standing between the self and everything else. Therefore, how one actually sees is transformed through such a lens. The discipline of being a Christian means that from now on I am to see each person not primarily in terms of ability, appearance, or usefulness, but as "the one for whom Christ died." Such a conversion inverts one's consciousness. Instead of my consciousness being a perspective of utility, of "I" dialoguing with "me" about our mutual self-interest, the dialogue is the mutuality of a Divine-human chattering—and that makes all the difference. As a result, simply to be conscious is to pray without ceasing.

As in all these exercises, one must set aside blocks of time for practice. Pianists practice daily so that on the night of the concert it is not they but the music that is heard. The serious runner so practices that on the afternoon of the race one runs as if it is second nature. So for the Christian, practice makes an activity so natural that there is no need to think about it. Thus the practice of consciousness as prayer requires sufficient rehearsal to make it second nature, until one unself-consciously lives dialogically.

3. *Intercessory Prayer as Contention*

The word prayer, as we have indicated, means "to ask." "Ask, and it will be given you" (Matt. 7:7). The Protestant Reformers focused their spirituality on this understanding. These were the times when they held up the face of the world's needs before the face of the God who in Jesus Christ promised redemptive companionship.

In so doing, they often used strong words, for to all appearances God was often derelict in regard to the promise to be good news for the poor, release for the captives, recovery of sight for the blind, and liberty for those who are oppressed. Far from being apologetic for their anger toward God, they insisted that prayer, to be genuine, *must* involve contention.

The psalmists knew this. Their vocabulary of prayer had at the top of the list words of anger, argument, begging, fighting, even cursing—accusing God of sleeping, betraying, being two-faced, unjust, even being on vacation. "I do not wonder, God," charged Teresa of Avila, "that you have so few friends from the way that you treat them." Ziggy gave the current equivalent. Looking up into the sky, he quietly asks, "Have you noticed, Sir, that the meek are still getting creamed?"

Prayer in this mode strives boldly to change God's mind, risking that in the exchange the same might happen to one's own self. Jacob wrestled with God, refusing to let go without a blessing, as will engaged Will. Likewise Job: "If [God] would slay me, . . . I should still argue my cause to [God's] face" (Job 13:15, author's translation). So it was with Jesus. Classic was his prayer in Gethsemane, that the cup would pass from him, contending with God with such fervor that his sweat was like drops of blood. Losing the confrontation the first time, he refused to acquiesce. He returned a second time, to no avail against a stubborn God. He refused the outcome. So a third time he reentered the contest, insisting on a reversed verdict. That should not be surprising, for in his teachings he had commended as a model for prayer the persistent widow badgering the judge. Even before that, he likened God to a neighbor, at whose door one needs to keep pounding if there is hope even of borrowing bread: "I tell you, though he will not get up and give him anything because he is his friend, yet because of his importunity he will rise and give him whatever he needs" (Luke 11:8).

> Lose the importunity of prayer, reduce it to soliloquy, or even to colloquy, with God, lose the real conflict of will and will, lose the habit of wrestling and the hope of prevailing with God, make it mere walking with God in friendly talk; and, precious as that is, yet you tend to lose the reality of prayer at last.[4]

This understanding of prayer is an important corrective to much contemporary piety. The Christian's stature should be an *adult* childlikeness, not a manger existence of parent-child docility, soaked in "wimpish," paternal, and shallow sentimentality. The relationship established by God's Incarnation is a *wedding*, beyond the point of all recall. Thus its most authentic testing is its capacity to withstand bitter contention—"for better, for worse." Such controversy is not nagging, which is simply compensation for inequality in relation. It is direct confrontation, rooted in the deepness of mutuality.

Loneliness can make life tedious and shopworn, a matter of indifference. But when one falls in love, especially with the Companion of Life itself, then all of life becomes sacred, and contention springs from passion. *Everything is unacceptable that defrauds or abuses life in any way, in part or in whole.* Thus, the more one experiences the companionship of God, the more one's pain at the condition of *our* world. And the more the pain, the more difficult it is to believe in the popular God, who supposedly rewards the just, punishes the unjust, and makes you feel delighted about the arrangement. Job is the definitive response: it simply is not so!

As an exercise, take careful notes during radio news, the five-minute kind that is broadcast every hour on the hour. When finished, rehearse the news with God. Imagine yourself in some of the situations reported. Picture persons by giving them names and faces. Feel dashed hopes, new possibilities—life, death, nothing, everything. Contend with God, letting the dialogue give free rise to thanksgiving, confession, accusation, commitment, reminding, promise. With Jesus as model, consider as possible test of true intercession one's willingness to become substitute for the hurting person for whom one is praying.

To take such prayer life seriously will no doubt lead to beginning a list of names of situations, groups, and persons for which one will take some responsibility. Lift these regularly in intercession to the face of God as promised Companion, with thankfulness, anger, hope, sorrow, promise, pleading. The promise to pray for someone is a weighty promise, never to be taken lightly. It is an unspoken responsibility of every pastor to pray regularly for each parishioner, by name, with face.

4. *Signs of Bonding*

Human relations thrive on signs of commitment, such as friendship, engagement, and wedding rings. A nun's veil is modeled after a bridal gown. Her vows are to Jesus, whom she marries for eternity, with even a honeymoon night as part of the spiritual consummation. Such signs are neither easily created nor quickly replaced. They participate in the special meaning of each particular relationship. Likewise, then, this spirit type thrives on tokens as reminders of one's Companion commitment. These may be a lapel pin, a cross around one's neck, a rosary in one's pocket, a picture in one's wallet, a special color that is "our" color. Symbols have power, so much so that few persons are able to have extramarital sex while wearing a wedding ring. Impossibly sentimental as it sounds, review in your memory the words of such love songs as "Together."

5. *Examination of Consciousness*

Incarnation is a name for the intersection of Divine and human, eternal with temporal. Too long have these dimensions been kept separate. To relate them, the church has long used a practice called "the examination of conscience." Wesley, for example, kept detailed records of his daily infractions and temptations. George Ashenbrenner, S.J., suggests that this practice has deteriorated from its original intent until it is now little more than moralistic self-indictment. He renames it the "examen of consciousness" in an effort to restore its meaning. Our spiritual blindness comes through failure to perceive the Divine intersections in the midst of our daily living. Thus we need a discipline for anticipating such incarnations, preparing ourselves to discern them concretely within our daily engagements in the marketplace.

To do this, he advocates a fifteen-minute morning prayer (perhaps with date book in hand) in which to walk through one's day, asking for discernment. One anticipates concrete opportunities, situations in which one might get "hooked," times of potential weakness, possible defensiveness that might later cause regret. During this period of preparation, the concretes of one's day become an interplay of faces and situations through spiritual imagination. When ready, one sets out to engage the world, more open and prepared to recognize the presence of the Divine in the "now," as the intersections actually occur.

At the end of the day, one conducts a spiritual review in reverse, remembering in thankfulness, confession, and insight the concrete intersections of Spirit with life that day. "Where did I see Christ today?" "When did I fail to be Christ to someone else?" Such examen may lead to a phone call of regret, a letter of invitation, a celebration by candlelight. Whatever one does, the purpose of such discipline is to make increasingly concurrent God's incarnational activity and one's responsive awareness.

If it be true that in as much "as you did it to one of the least of these . . . , you did it to me," an important exercise is to make a conscious effort to see Christ in some designated place, such as an airport. Look carefully at random faces passing on the escalator, smile back at a child's giggle, wave at the sounds of happy hour, surprise with a greeting those looking hassled. Perform at least one act that is sensitive to the Divine vicariousness. Risk being misunderstood—as when an offer to carry a suitcase may be received as an overture to "mugging."

6. *Guided Imagery*

Jesuit spirituality, following the lead of Saint Ignatius of Loyola, centers in the use of memory and imagination as a way of becoming incarnated within key biblical scenes. By using as many senses as possible, one walks into a biblical situation, reconstructing it as a "composition of place." Such "discursive meditation" is evoked by asking questions. What is Jesus feeling as he looks over his shoulder and sees Judas? Picture the scene. How many are there? Smell the sweat, the torches. What would you do if you were Peter? On and on, let the images flow as you "get into it," and the parts and the whole begin to speak to each other.

"Have this mind among yourselves, which is yours in Christ Jesus" (Phil. 2:5)—or Mary Magdalene, or the child set in Jesus' presence, or the Mary pondering "all these things in her heart." Whichever scene one chooses, Ignatius' final questions come down to three: What have I done for Christ; what am I doing for Christ; what am I going to do for Christ?[5]

As a variation of this exercise, choose a biblical situation, preferably one that parallels your own feelings about your present situation. Read the story quickly to get the general story line. What is it? Then read the story again, as if you are the stage manager in charge of creating the scenery. What do you propose? Read it a third time, more slowly. Enter each character as if you are the director in charge of part casting. What kind of a person do you need to find for each part? What will you have the applicants do to see if they are right for the part? Do you know any persons who would be "naturals" for the parts? Then read the story a final time, as if you are the drama critic watching your own opening-night production. What is your version really about? Who is the star? When you finish, close the Bible and ask yourself, Which of these parts am I actually playing in my daily life? Then, What role would I most like? And finally, What do I need to do to try out for the part?

A guided Ignatian Retreat of thirty days (or the more recently developed nine-day version) is a valuable way of using this method for traversing the sweep of salvation history. If this is impossible or unavailable, one can construct one's own retreat. Set aside at least a day to go apart. Divide the time available into seven equal parts, each part having a time for scripture reading, for quiet savoring of that experience, and for a walk or some exercise as a "break" between each of the seven segments. Use the imaginative technique suggested above, having with you only a Bible, a notebook, and a pencil. The suggested readings are these:

> Creation—Genesis 1:1–2:3
> Abraham's Sacrifice—Genesis 22:1–14
> Exodus—Exodus 14:15–31
> The Longing for God—Psalm 42

Vision of the Covenant Renewed—Isaiah 55:1–11
The Promise Fulfilled—Luke 4:14–30
The Mission—John 21:1–17

A longer "framing retreat" is possible by recognizing that the church year is divided into two parts, with a common three-phase rhythm to each: promise, fulfillment, mission. Thus we have the period of Advent-Christmas-Epiphany, and that of Lent-Easter-Pentecost. Choose one of these periods. Select key scripture readings for each of the three phases (use a concordance). Using a calendar, establish a set daily or weekly time schedule for doing specific guided imagery. Consider the best setting and symbols for each passage.

A more open-ended variation is to use biblical themes symbolically. Take yourself on a directed tour of your house in search of the lost coin. Where did you finally find it? What is it? Why was it lost? What will you do not to lose it again? Try the pearl of great price, the exodus, Abraham's call to sacrifice what was most sacred, the rich young ruler's question to Jesus, "What must I do?"[6] Such guided imagery can be made very open-ended, as in having little more instruction than: "You are walking down a road and meet someone. You imagine it from there." Or the scene can be one of finding yourself before a closed door, or finding an old chest in the attic.

7. The Imitation of Christ

Luther forcefully insisted that the center of Christian faith is "not to know of any God except the one who was made flesh." While orthodoxy does this by focusing on Christ *for* us, and pietism favors Christ *in* us, there is also a strong spiritual strand that claims Christ *with* us. Protestants tend to understand this mode as the call to "follow Christ," while Roman Catholics speak more often of it as "imitating Christ." "I have given you an example" (John 13:15). "Permit me," pleaded the early martyr St. Ignatius of Antioch, "to be an imitator of my suffering God."

Saint Francis understood such role-modeling this way. Being created in the image of God, we can know what we are created to be by imitating the life of Jesus, who is God. Therefore he took literally Jesus' call to take no gold, bag, sandals, or staff, and only one tunic (Matt. 10:9–10). So deeply did he participate in such spirituality that the imitation became literal—receiving stigmata marks of crucifixion on his hands and feet.

Living one's life as incarnation means the service of self-emptying, but not to get something, not because one "should." It is a response anchored in thankfulness for what God has already done. I have already been given all that really matters.

Literal imitation is different from literalistic modeling. Jesus wants not copies but disciples. In fact, we do not even know precisely what Jesus was like, but we can sense what it might mean to follow him through a Francis who walked with him daily. Thus for the world to see Christ, nothing more should be needed than to "see how these Christians love one another" (Tertullian). Even persons for whom orthodox Christology is problematic find a powerful spiritual attraction in the exemplary Jesus whose gentle charisma of presence is contagious.

There is evidence that from the nineteenth century to the present this spirit mode has been central for the serious Christian:

> To imitate Christ, to follow Him, to be conformed to Him, to cling to Him, to live as He did and with Him—these are the recurring aspirations in the spiritual writings of the century, in retreats, preaching, and devotional practices.[7]

Charles de Foucauld has not only provided for this mode a selection of Gospel texts called *The Unique Model,* but so gave his own life that he became a model of the practice. In a letter to the Poor Clares at Nazareth, he described his approach:

> In order to be entirely detached from yourself, to forget oneself totally and to be concerned in all things with God's glory, the best way seems to be to ask yourself constantly what Jesus would think, say, or do in your place and then to think, say, and do what He would do. . . . That is why He came to dwell among us, so that we might always have an easy way, available to all, to practice perfection: we have only to look at Him and do as He does.[8]

With Jesus' dictum, "Follow me," came the invitation, "Come and see." Thus, command and companionship belong together. So in Paul, the command to "have this mind . . . which is yours in Christ," has as its glad underside the affirmation that "it is no longer I who live, but Christ who lives in me" (Gal. 2:20). The example is *of* Christ and *for* Christ, but because it is *with* Christ and *in* Christ. In this sense, Jesus is the "first-born among many" (Rom. 8:29).

Whatever form one's exercises take in attempting this *imitatio Christi*, they need to arise through meditation upon the person and actions of Christ as found in the Gospels. The simplest experiment is the method we described from Charles de Foucauld, or more popularly adapted to Protestant piety by Charles Sheldon's *In His Steps*.[9] The practice begins by setting aside a section of one's day in which periodically to ask: What would Jesus think, say, and do now in this situation? Then think, say, and do it—now. If one cannot handle an extended period of time, begin with a manageable segment. One hour at a time. How about fifteen minutes?

One weakness in this practice as it is sometimes lived is to take too narrow an episode in Jesus' life as application to too large a slice of ours. For example, one could mistakenly take the Jesus who said, "The poor you always have with you" as a basis for imagining Jesus' opposition to social restructuring in behalf of the oppressed. The Jesus of this spirit type dare not be one pulled piecemeal into the present, complete with club lapel emblem, upward mobility, and a multi-cable TV. The Jesus here must be a composite one, gained as a whole from the full Gospels, from manger beginning to outcast ending—the one who taught less by dictum than by imaginative parable, of which he himself was the primary one.

For those who find the whole of Jesus' life an impossible or inaccessible model, an insight by Kierkegaard is promising. Somewhere in his journal he wrote that to understand oneself is to see what God really wishes one to do. Kierkegaard's point can be distilled into one assignment: "to find a truth which is true for me, to find the idea for which I can live and die." Paul's answer was this: "To live is Christ, and to die is gain" (Phil. 1:21).

As an exercise, focus on one period of Jesus' life, or one episode, or one parable, perhaps one that parallels your own present situation. Let it fasten itself onto you so that it becomes the idea for which you live for a set period of time. As a variation, choose a period, episode, or story from your own life, and distill the truth or idea for which you seemed then to be living. With practice, raise the difficult question: What of the present?

Consult a concordance, looking under the alphabetically listed themes for passages that touch your own present pain, anxiety, struggle. Take the passages in disciplined order, using one of the methods mentioned above. You will discover that bringing your particularized need to scripture focuses your ability to see. Amos Wilder's identification of all Gospel stories as variations on the theme of "lost and found" says as much about him as it does about scripture.[10]

An interesting approach is to read literature that deals with the theme of the imitation of Christ. Two novels that reflect something of the powerful options are: Bernanos, *Diary of a Country Priest*, and Kazantzakis, *The Last Temptation of Christ*.[11] The recent motion picture *Jesus of Montreal* is an unusually provocative portrayal of this theme.

We often forget the full humanness of Jesus, "one who in every respect has been tempted as we are" (Heb. 4:15). As you read scripture, keep a list of passages in which Jesus identifies with the difficult times likely to occur in your own life. Then live with an appropriate passage when such a time occurs. These passages may help as a beginning:

- Abused/rejected: Mark 6:3; Luke 4:28–30; 11:53–54; 16:14; 17:25; 18:32–34; 20:20; 21:12–19; 22:33–34, 47–65; 23:1–5; John 15:18–27
- Alone: Matt. 14:13; Mark 1:35; Luke 8:19–21
- Disappointed: Matt. 11:16–19; Mark 10:17–22; Luke 13:31–35; 17:11–19
- Angry/hated: Matt. 12:34; 23:13–39; Mark 3:1–6; 10:13–16; 11:12–19; Luke 9:55; 11:42–54; 13:14–17; 14:26–27
- Desire/affection: Luke 7:36–50; 22:14–16; John 13:23; 20:11–18; 21:20
- Destitute: Matt. 20:26–27; Luke 9:57–62
- Fear/troubled: Mark 14:32–42; 15:16–20; Luke 22:40–46; John 12:27; 13:21
- Inadequacy: Luke 18:19
- Overwhelmed: Mark 3:20–21; 6:30–34; 7:24
- Sad: Matt. 26:37–38; Luke 13:33–35; 19:41–42; 22:60–62; John 11:35
- Suffering: Mark 13:9–13; Luke 9:22–27
- Tempted: Matt. 4:1–11; 26:39–46; Luke 17:1

Encouraged by such a list, begin your own summary of the positive aspects of Jesus' humanity. Be sure not to forget his love of eating and drinking, his joy in the little things, his passion for deep friendships, and his sly sense of humor.

8. *Beginning and Ending the Day*

In college, I had a roommate who greeted the alarm clock with a curse. I simply got used to his language, failing to see the impact it had on beginning my day. The awareness came at a prayer center, when I was awakened with the startling Easter words every morning: "Christ has risen!" "Amen!" I responded, without thinking. The contrast with "Damn!" was clear.

As an exercise, memorize a passage to repeat immediately upon awaking, and another for just before falling asleep. A morning one that comes to mind is Psalm 118:24:

> This is the day which the Lord has made;
> Let us rejoice and be glad in it.

For evening, a simple one from Compline is, "Into your hands, Lord, I commend my spirit." (See Luke 23:26.) If something more developed is desired, the following are mine, to which you are welcome. Place them on a card by your bed until you can create something especially your own.

For the morning:

> Yours is the day, O God, and yours is the night.
> You have established the sun and the moon.
> It is you who have fixed the boundaries of the earth;
> summer and winter you have made.
> Parent of the orphan, lover of the widow,
> you give the lonely a home, and lead prisoners to freedom.
> May I walk with you this day?

For the evening:

> You are in our midst, O Lord, your name we bear.
> Do not forsake us, O Yahweh, our God.
> Into your hands I commend my spirit.
> If I live, I live to the Lord; if I die, I die to the Lord.
> So whether I live or die, I am the Lord's.
> Into your hands I commend my spirit.
> Keep me as the apple of your eye,
> protect me in the shadow of your wings;
> undergird me with your everlasting arms.
> Into your hands I commend my spirit.
> May the Almighty God grant us a quiet night,
> and a peaceful end.

9. *The Eucharist*

Christians who belong to a "high-church" denomination are blessed in having the Eucharist available frequently, as an empowering reenactment of the Incarnation. It is revealing that on Maundy Thursday evening, Protestants tend to see Communion as a sad remembrance—of the *Last* Supper. Roman Catholics, on the other hand, celebrate it as a time of joy—as the *Lord's* Supper. From the latter perspective, the One who was about to be taken away instituted the Eucharist as an ongoing event of Real Presence. "I will not leave you desolate; I will come to you" (John 14:18). The One who invites to the Table is also the nourishment. The storyteller becomes the story.

A young monk, having a hard time in his struggle to find God, was given this advice by his spiritual director: "Quit searching. After Eucharist each morning, sit quietly and savor the fact that with the bread and wine the incarnation has just reoccurred—in you. The Presence is within."

10. *Storytelling*

Storytelling is being rediscovered not only as an art form but as an important approach to theology.[12] One reason for this is the power of metaphor to evoke meaning in an age such as ours— reduced by quantity and efficiency to the literal. I have twin daughters. Years ago, when they came home after a movie, our conversations were markedly different. "What was it about?" From one, I received a blow-by-blow account, a process that took almost as long as the movie. When she finished, I would ask, "That's what happened; now what was it about?" She couldn't handle the question. "I just told you!" The other twin would tell a story. "Do you remember the time we climbed Mt. Sopris, and weren't sure we could make it—but the crazy dog from next door got there before we did, and was waiting at the top? Well, that's kind of what this movie's about." "What do you mean?" would come the frustrated retort from the other twin, "there wasn't even a dog in the movie!"

The writers of the Bible were largely editors. Out of the countless stories told around campfires about Israel's past, they chose a "story of stories." "Want to know what Israel's history is all about? Well, once upon a time there was a garden. . . ." The rest of the Old Testament supplied the names of the various characters who, from time to time, took on the role of "apple pickers." "Do you want to know who is God?" Jesus, in effect, asked. "Well, once there was a father with two sons. . . ."

As an exercise, choose a partner. The task is to ask each other questions, with the only acceptable answer being a story serving as a story of stories. For example, what story would you tell to answer the question, "Who were you as a child?" Or "How do you remember your mother?" Keep getting harder questions. "What do you make of your life thus far?" When you are ready for the advanced course, the graduate question is: "Who is God?"

Life teaches how close sadness and humor can be. Humans are blessed, as Israel well knew, with the ability to tell stories about the difficult past so as to redeem it with laughter. A favorite disaster story in our family starts this way: "Remember the time we hiked to Geneva Lake, and the rains moved in. And it turned out the plastic sheet we took for a tent had holes in it, and all we had to mend it were dried out Band-Aids. And we tried to cook beans with a candle, and someone sat on the sandwiches. . . ." By this point in the story, the laughter is infectious. As an exercise, choose a past event that was difficult or disappointing for you. Tell it to a friend, experiencing the redemptive distance that comes through the companionship of shared story.

11. *Meditation*

Among words worth gathering for centered attention in this spirit type are these: covenant, Emmanuel, with, incarnate, for, Abba, companion, presence, eucharist, relationship, contention, communion, dialogue, engagement, wedding.

12. *Music*

For one's collection of music capable of rehearsing this spirit mode, one might consider these compositions: Haydn's *The Seven Last Words of Christ on the Cross*, Wagner's Prelude to *Parsifal*, and Bach's *St. Matthew Passion*.

13. *Painting*

The spirituality of type 5 is captured brilliantly by Rembrandt.[13] His figures are etched by a mysterious light, promising to humanness a gentleness born of suffering. Here resurrection appears as hint, experienced as a "nevertheless," because the Divine has taken up housekeeping and dwelt among us. The miracle of incarnation as companion presence can be recognized in his work simply in the fact that the tragic sufferings of soul cannot extinguish the sacredness of another realm, come near. The beauty to which the gospel gives birth is sad and tender, a scarred but deep integrity, of such endurance that it will be faithful to the end. Through the eyes honed by his paintings, one can imagine what it might mean to see each person as the one for whom Christ died. A rare sensitivity for this spirit mode of Divine-human companionship can be gained by placing, side-by-side, Rembrandt's *Christ at Emmaus* with one of his many self-portraits.

A Summary

As we have seen, this mode can be tasted in various ways. Some persons sense it when the darkness takes on a "feel" of warm presence. For others, it becomes real when the I-me babbling of consciousness becomes an I-Thou dialogue, rendering one's stream of consciousness a praying without ceasing. For still others, it emerges as Brother Lawrence's sense of prayer as a shared familiarity of the heart. Whatever its form, the Companion closer than breath itself is the acknowledgment that we will never again be alone: "I will not leave you desolate; I will come to you" (John 14:18).

The Incarnation is God's commitment that "we are in it together." Such togetherness is far more than proximity. It is a relation of immersion, ingression, infusion. From our side, insists Brother Lawrence, the love affair entails a reckless throwing of ourselves into the arms of infinite love, "a total and universal abandonment of oneself into [God's] hands, without worrying what will become of one after death."[14] This is because, in the incarnation, God has already thrown God's self recklessly into our arms. Herein resides the basis for preposterous trust.

This spirit mode provides as much an answer to the problem of evil as we are likely to get. In facing the relentless assault of leukemia, for instance, everything depends on one question: Is the crucifixion actually the agony of the Incarnate One? If so, then Christ's scream of abandonment on the cross is a Divine legacy, signed in blood, that death and evil are not part of God's design. *They are God's enemies too.* Camus's agnosticism rested on one lament: "If only the cosmos like us could love, we would be reconciled."[15] Jesus Christ is the declaration that this is incredibly so. In the crucifixion we behold both the center of history and the heart of God, in intersection. God's "no" against death is God's steadfast "yes" for life—to be experienced in a fullness that acknowledges spirit life as richly pluralistic.

8

Homesickness and the Hunger for Integrity

Type 6: Craving

The spirit type to which we now turn relates to type 4, but in an inverted way. As we saw, awareness of contingency brings a desert spirituality, emerging as profound humility. Here, however, that sense of fragility births a hunger. One becomes bitten by an unshakable persistence, a sense of homesickness, for something one hardly knows how to name. It comes of realizing finally that *one can never truly be satisfied with anything finite.* One senses hints of this as a child, perhaps in the pain of going away to summer camp for the first time. But here, in spirit type 6, that wistfulness is for a place I've never seen before. Language pales into abstraction, but the homesickness is a yearning for adoption, for a final belonging.

Some taste this at the end of a typical day, characterized by compromise. On the way home, one yearns for integrity. There is a strange hunger to feel at home, truly, at least with one's self. But where it gets scary is in reaching a point of no return, where I can no longer fool myself with a can of beer and a promise to do better tomorrow. There comes a moment when I know that no matter how much I try, there will always be about my life a "not-quite-everness." Quest, nostalgia, reaching, homesickness—these are the marks of an exile. I am "in," but now I know that I can never be fully "of," no matter what. There's a line over which I cannot go without losing myself. There is a Game in which my game is being played, with rules not of my making. Somehow life is not as much on my terms as I once thought

Erikson described the stage of life characterizing older adults as slung between the options of despair and the search for integrity. Sometimes this dilemma comes much earlier in life.

Absence as Presence

There is a positive side to this mode, suggested by the fact that we are describing the Spirit as *Redeemer*. What this means is that this apparent absence that gnaws is, in truth, a Presence. *Our restlessness is God's doing*. The more lonely the office after hours, the more clear one's inability to be satisfied by Madison Avenue promises, the more that compromise feels cheap even if no one knows, then the closer one is to this spirit mode—as personal haunting.

Robert Frost wrote of two diverging roads in a wood.[1] This spirit type is about the one "less traveled by." To be brought to understand why that "made all the difference" is to discover that the Holy Spirit as redemptive means God as *Pursuer*. The good news follows, but not quickly. At work here is the Divine determination never to let us rest in our inauthenticity.

This mode means coming face to face with God as the hound of heaven. God is the one whose resolve is to leave nothing unturned in the search for the lost coin—which is me, and you. Thus the restless Spirit will not stay put, but keeps leaving the ninety and nine for the plus one.

Gentle Ferociousness

Sometimes folks have trouble with this mode because it threatens to banish one's former God to the garage. Having one's heels bitten by pursuit makes one painfully aware that the "gentleman God" is intolerably bourgeois. We are no longer dealing here with a God whose low-key sales pitch provides polite options for personal tastes. The God here is not even courteous—the one who telephones before making house calls, or knocks once and leaves. The God of "if you please" is swept away by the Pursuer whose only tactics are to knock your door in or utterly pass you by— which, one finally comes to see, has the same intent.

Francis Thompson's classic poem "The Hound of Heaven" distills this mode. What we hear are Feet that follow "with unhurrying chase,/And unperturbèd pace," which make sounds that "speak by silences," and "find me stripped in sleep."

> I stand amid the dust o' the mounded years—
> My mangled youth lies dead beneath the heap.

My days have crackled and gone up in smoke, . . .
Yea, faileth now even dream.[2]

Finally comes the confession. I admit to myself "how little worthy of any love." Yet to no avail. I feel beneath even this beginning honesty that which continues to strip away. And someday I may dare to pause for a moment and look behind. Then may I sense that it is "not for thy harms." Instead, the pursuit is so that I might come to know the Pursuer as, in fact, the One "Whom thou seekest!" And the name? The "tremendous Lover."[3]

To Be Bitten

Kierkegaard claims that each of us has only one task, requiring a lifetime: "To become who you are." For this task, he claims, there are "stages along life's way," along which we are pursued. One is forced to leap from threshold to threshold, not so much "to" as "from"—exiting that living which keeps becoming unlivable. Made to yearn for one's true self, one is forced to keep peeling off the illusions, until someday one discovers the outer edges of that self which is the product of God's yearning throughout.

Such pursuit is multi-edged. One can experience it as being prodded from behind, as being lured from in front, or as hemorrhaging from within. Kierkegaard's language is of having salt rubbed into open sores, while at the same time being wounded from behind. Whatever the situation, more becomes less, and less becomes a locked door leading nowhere. And as one's joys take on a melancholy edge, it happens. The edge becomes tantalizing. It is like seasoning, whetting one's taste for "the more" as "beyond," the "not yet" as "if only."

At each point in our pilgrimage, there will be many things willing to apply for the job of satisfying every longing. But the letters of recommendation have one of three conjunctions in each sentence— "but," "although," or "yet." In coming to know this, one comes to know far more.

And what "more" does one know? I know that one November my parents kept talking about sleds. "Don has a nice one." "Looks like snow; too bad you don't have a sled." I felt tormented. We couldn't afford one. Even if we could, I didn't deserve one. Christmas Eve it snowed. I went to bed, deliciously miserable. Would I get one? Of course not! But would they have pursued me like that if they didn't have something in mind? When I awoke, it was still snowing. I went down to the Christmas tree. The sled was red.

The Reversal

Can it be that this spirit type is as unusually available in our time as it is unsuspected? What an important reversal if folks could come to sense that the yearnings rampant in our culture, birthed by unhappiness, frustration, anxiety, and unfulfilledness, are in truth the workings of God! Then one would sense the strange One, whose motive in pursuing is the precise opposite of the way it feels.

EXERCISES

1. *Recollection*

Recollection is a time in which to do for the soul what the monthly balancing of the checkbook does for one's financial affairs. It is when the phrase "What's the bottom line?" is applied to one's spiritual life. When I worked in a bank, we used a form called a "recapitulation statement." That was a fancy name for a withdrawal slip, intent on recollecting how much one had in one's account from which to draw. Such "recapitulation" is a regular necessity in one's spirit life.

As indicated by the chart, such an exercise involves discernment of Spirit through the redemptive mode. It works best through questions. Where was there cause for celebration in the Spirit's workings with me over the past month? Where was there weakness to which I need to respond with focused resolve? Whereas in the financial realm such helps as checkbook and monthly statements are provided, one must create one's own equivalents for recollecting one's spirituality.

"Nine Questions" is an exercise that can be used for either personal or group recollection. Take a piece of paper and a pencil. Limit yourself to ten seconds for answering each question, although you may take longer time between questions. The purpose is to take yourself by surprise, much as an unannounced bank auditor.

1. In order to distill how you are feeling now, what color comes to mind as "being you"?
2. With what biblical character do you most identify right now?
3. With what animal would other persons tend to associate you? Which would you choose as appropriate?
4. If you could go to any city in the world, which one would most appeal to you?
5. If a friend asks you for an object that reflects what it is like to live inside you, which object would you choose?
6. What kind of building would be most appropriate for having housed you this past month? Which room in that building?
7. Where would you go if you were given an afternoon of unexpected free time?
8. What would you do there?
9. With whom would you do it?

First consider prayerfully your separate answers and then your answers taken as a unified statement. Use a "third eye" for what, goaded on by Spirit, your secret self might be shyly hinting. Sharing such an exercise with a friend over coffee is helpful. Just as resolves are needed concerning what a checkbook reveals, so here.

Consider two additional exercises in recollection. Using your checkbook, review your expenditures for the month. Record them on a chart of your own creation. One possibility would be to draw three lines across the page, labeled physical, intellectual, spiritual. Then draw columns with such headings as "me," "family," "friends," "strangers," "causes," "church," and so on. Fill in the squares with the appropriate figures. Some expenditures may fit in more than one category. When finished, total the columns. Reflect on the meaning of the amounts, frequency, priorities, and rhythm.

As a second exercise, take your "little black book" or daily calendar for the past month. Do the same as above with your activities. What does your "doing" tell you about who you are?

2. Journaling

There are as many ways of journaling as there are persons.[4] Find the method that best suits you. A journal is not a diary, or record. It is a vehicle for dialogue. It records the currents operative in the flow of your life, so that you can discern the rocks, the intersections, the sparkling of the ripples, the overhanging branches, the channels of possibilities, and the direction of the current. While its form is primarily that of dialogue between "I" and "me," its meaning comes through a discernment belonging to spirit with Spirit.

Acquire the tools for journaling that are right for you. Some find that a bound book with blank pages works well, being symbolic of how seriously they vow to take the task, how sacred they wish to hold themselves, and how cherished over the years they promise to regard the results. Personally, I get inhibited by such a book form. It seems to filter what I write, for who can babble into a volume bound for "eternity"? I even prefer a pencil to a pen, giving me further permission to be "tentative." I use a looseleaf notebook. This gives me flexibility to take out pages for comparison, or, on occasion, to share with someone whose insights I value, such as a spiritual director.

Take precautions to ensure that your journal remains private. Wesley used a code. Most people hide or lock it in a special place. I mislabel my journal and shelve it among academic notebooks. Its present noninviting title is "Lectures in Metaphysics."

What follows are some suggestions that work for me. I usually am unable to write daily. Writing every three days or so seems sufficient for me. I divide each journal page by drawing a line down the middle. On the left side, I make regular entries. On the right, I record any discernments that come anytime later in rereading what I wrote, gaining perspective through distance.

A second section of my journal is marked "Month." Each month, I set aside time to reread carefully my entries for that month, plus additional insights recorded along the way. I record my new discernments on the left side, reserving the right for any further ones gained through rereading the previous month's discernments. A third section is marked "Insights." Here I record anything that somehow deserves special consideration, to be dealt with "sometime." A fourth section is a "Dream and Fantasy Log."

Then once a year, usually on New Year's Eve, I go apart and reread the entries made for each of the months of the year. The insights gained are recorded on the left side of a section marked "Year." Then I reread the entries covering the past several years. I look for patterns, breakthroughs, persistent yearnings, stepping-stones, unresolved warnings, opportunities. In so doing, I let myself be swept by the lullabies and nudgings of the one known as Pursuer.

When finished, the discernments gained are offered up in the context of Wesley's Watchnight liturgy, ending with a concrete rededication of life for the next year.[5] Some persons might prefer that overall reviews and rededications be done more often, perhaps tied to the church year, as at the beginning of Advent and on Ash Wednesday.

3. *Dreams*

It is remarkable how often scripture records God's disclosures as occurring through dreams—from Jacob's famous ladder into heaven, to the saving of the baby Jesus from slaughter through a dream warning. Jung's work has helped many persons today use dreams as vehicles for spiritual wholeness. Some persons interpret dreams narrowly, as if a direct message is intended. Most therapists agree that dreams "say something," but their "language" is metaphorical. Wholeness is enabled by discerning the intent of their "pursuit."[6] My personal experience is that they have multiple meanings, to be experienced more as invitations for exploration than commands for obedience.

A widespread problem in using dreams is our tendency to forget them, almost immediately. At best, most dreams do not last in the conscious memory for more than a quarter of an hour after awakening. Thus, keep paper and pencil beside your bed so that you can record a dream as soon as possible. Never rely on memory. Record images, faces, colors, feelings, locations, sounds. Then, when you have unhurried time, treat the dream as you would a poem—for it is, in fact, an uncanny distillation of the symbols out of which your spirituality is being birthed. It is not by accident that dreams of pursuit are an abundant part of the itinerary of most persons' dreams.

Each of us is a dreamer, and all dreamers are poets. Share your dream-poems with a friend. Together, sharpen your sensitivity for repetitions, themes, persistent characters, and common plots. Once one is captured by the metaphor of a dream, the meaning unfolds itself.[7] Use the chart for the nine spirit modes as a framework for classifying dreams, in each case looking with the triune eyes of was, is, and shall be. Practice in tromping around in the corridors of one's dreams is one of the best ways to become a theological adventurer.

One can actually choose the subject of one's dream drama. To do this, isolate an issue. Write it down, providing enough detail to lock in its anatomy as a theme. Place the pad by your bed. As you are passing into sleep, use as a mantra a question that poses your issue. For example, "Shall I go?" Immediately upon waking, write down not only your dreams, but everything that comes to mind. Reject nothing as irrelevant. Later reread what you wrote, praying for discernment.

4. *The Healing of Memories*

This healing exercise is one of the most necessary, yet painful, of all the spiritual exercises of this mode. It must be done carefully, when you are ready, with a fairly clear sense of your present emotional limits. Make sure that a sensitive friend is available, or, preferably, have telephone access to a spiritual director or therapist whose work you trust. The task is to reopen in the presence of the Spirit some of the deeper pains of the past, so as to enable the redemptive work of Spirit. The process involved entails far more than gaining insights about the past. It is a profound spiritual experience of *reliving the past with new company.*

Much of the pain by which each of us is scarred began when we were young, when we were particularly vulnerable in our loneliness. Indelible is my own image of being a skinny only child, feeling terribly alone on the first-grade playground as teams were "picked up" for a game. I was chosen last, and, as I recall it, grudgingly. The center of the Christian disclosure, grounded in the Incarnation, is the good news that *never again will I be alone*—not even on the playground! Companionship, as the declared center point of history, is a promise having to do with *now*. The Pursuer insists that "where I am you may be also." Thus even Christ's "going away" is a gift: "I will send you a Comforter" (John 16:7, author's paraphrase). The Spirit as Redeemer is that promised healer. This exercise is a trusting that it is so.

Thus, if I truly believe that I am no longer alone, I can go back onto that grade-school playground, through the side door that I have kept chained for years. And, behold, it is different. With the supportive distance of such Companionship that has chosen me, I can deeply relive that very event. There is courage even to open one's cellar door, as it were, behind which at night chains can be heard to rattle. With such companionship even the most disturbing sounds can come to resemble mice with megaphones.

- For this exercise, set aside some open-ended time, or at least some carefully protected segments. Using a pencil and paper, begin with "roving prayer." With the Spirit, rove over the journey of your life. Note what events seem to divide your pilgrimage into segments, perhaps five or more of them. Give them names. Then rove over each of them in turn, using a separate page. List things as quickly as they come to you. Underline the key episodes. Encourage your memory by focusing on:

> Loss: persons, things, events
> Regrets: roads taken, not chosen, unrecognized, unwanted
> Frights: real, anticipated, dreaded
> Guilts: for things received, things done, things suspected

The task, at this point, is not to do anything with this material. The task is to get it out, all out—an emotional inventory, as it were.

- When ready, which may be a different time, choose one of these periods of your life. I suggest the one that feels most painful, mysterious, or enigmatic. Use your notes as a base. The intent is to understand what Gandhi meant in identifying prayer as the poor person's medicine. There can be no healing without lancing the wounds.
- After choosing a particular period, finish the task of getting it "out of your system." Keep writing whatever comes. The task at this stage is to gather the puzzle pieces. The more one records, the more will remembrances emerge from rooms unrecognized. By analogy, remember the frustration of working a puzzle with missing pieces.
- When this unburdening process slows, it is time to see that the pieces are turned right side up, beginning the search for those which suggest borders, corners, significant figures, objects, and color combinations. The first step in this process is one of *acknowledgment*, the second that of *understanding*. At either stage, do not try to do anything to this material. That would be like forcing pieces to fit. Let the repetitions, patterns, and themes speak and arrange themselves, with you as midwife.
- Useful throughout this process is the image of one's life as a tree. At the beginning, one roves the surface of the leaves, recognizing the branches from which they are growing. Then one discerns the various branches that together form a limb. In time, the dynamic moves toward the roots. Yet even in the limbs, one can often discern hints of the roots. Keep drawing

connections as you go deeper. The roots will not be sufficiently plumbed until you reach those few taproots which are basic to your spiritual, emotional, and physical nutrition and malnutrition.

- These taproot themes will be intertwined around one or more concrete events. Although they may be small in time or action, they function in primal ways. They are like symbols that distill and rehearse patterns of action and interaction. Expressed another way, they are replayable tapes which get turned on too easily by "hooks" in the present. As a result, they not only threaten one's equilibrium, but strain one's relationships, projecting onto others the emotional baggage stored up for someone else. Turn over innocent-looking rocks, checking for scorpions of rejection, abandonment, depression, insecurity, fear, and violation. Let the doors creak open. See if their sounds echo and reecho along the corridors of your life memory. Feel the musty air, strangely luminous with faces and names and smells of yesterday, and this morning, and tonight.

- Crucial throughout, however, is to remember and rehearse the fact that you are no longer alone. This is not a remembering of how it felt *then*. It is a reliving of how it feels *now*. Brother Lawrence's "practice of the presence" is helpful. Babble and share all of this with the Spirit as redemptive companion: "Look at that, now!" "Can you make anything out of this connection?"

- In time, you will be ready for the next stage, which is *understanding* moving toward *forgiveness*. In the presence of the Pursuer now Friend, examine the taproot events that you have discerned. Notice that there are two types, usually related. The first is easiest to recognize. Its barometer is *guilt*. This type has to do with things I have done, and do, as variations of a persistent tendency. The "aha" is recognizable: "There it is. Every time I get in that situation, I lash out in an effort to . . ." "Mary, forgive me. John, Susan . . . God!"

- Such acknowledgment involves far more than receiving a clean slate. That would simply tidy up the environment for making old errors in new ways. With your finger on the pulse of the cause, see it through to its *healing*. What one must be released from is self-inflicted punishment, as if atonement could come through writing phrases of unworthiness on the chalkboard of one's mind, over and over again. Since the diagnosis is being made on a formative level, one is well on the way to understanding the "why" and thus the interconnect-edness of one's actions. It is on this level that redemption must be experienced—through acceptance as forgiveness, the lack of which has been a primal cause.

> God, knowing now some of the factors of why I do what I do, forgive me. Heal me of my low self-image, that I may see myself as you do—as a pearl of great price. Amen.

This request must have response as its other side.

> Though my sins be as scarlet, you can make them as white as snow. In the name of Jesus Christ, I accept myself as forgiven and washed clean. May I pick up my bed and walk. Amen.

The second type of taproot events often go still deeper. These have *anger* as their barometer. If you need additional support during this phase, surround yourself with tokens of the Divine companionship. This type is especially difficult for the Christian who, having been taught to see anger as wrong, has learned well how to hide it. But having been forgiven for the hurts that one has done, one has permission to confess that which has been *done unto oneself.*

- Refrain from explanations, rationalizations, and justifica-tions: "My mother was trying to do the best she could." Cut out all such qualifications. Feel it deeply, and state it straight: "The bottom line is that she hurt me, badly—like the time . . ." Vomit it out, for these are the scars cover-ing the infection, reoccurring for years as a scaly rash, evoked at the most unexpected times by folks often well-intentioned.
- As part of this process, one might write a letter to one or more of the persons involved, whether alive or dead. The need is self-clarity through self-emptying, not necessarily a commu-nication to be sent. The goal is to work through the pain to the other side, a point finally recognizable by the words, "Now I understand." "All my life, all I ever really wanted was to hear her say, 'I love you.' But she never did, and I've been trying to earn it ever since!" There may even come the un-derstanding that "She didn't because she couldn't. All *she* ever wanted to hear was *her father* saying the same words, which he never said, maybe because . . ."
- Do not hurry this process. There can never be a good lawn without digging up the rusty tin cans over which the devel-

oper has placed a thin layer of topsoil. It may take hours, days, weeks. But there will come a transition when one will be able to say: "Father, forgive them, for they knew not what they were doing. They were doing unto others as they had been done unto, like the sins of the fathers and mothers unto the third and fourth generations." But even then, the process is not done. The final stage, strangely, is *thankfulness*. The irony is that many of the memories needing healing have also been roots for one's most special qualities. This means thankfulness not for the motivations involved, but for the secondary and often unintended results. Thus, for example, one's experience of abandonment may have birthed one's sensitivity to serve the outcasts of society. Or the words "You can't do anything right!" may in actuality have been what energized one's defiant determination to succeed. For better or worse—and now one can begin to see "for better"—one is what one is because of one's spotty past.

To be forgiven and to forgive, then, is the process of healing memories, in four stages: Acknowledgment—Understanding—Forgiveness—Thankfulness.[8]

Another exercise that can either follow or precede the healing of memories is the writing of a "theological autobiography." This is not a record of spiritual experiences or religious matters. It is an attempt to distill from the common-day experiences composing one's life those hinge points of meaning which render existence a pilgrimage. The Hebrew scripture is precisely that: Israel's telling of stories in an effort to discern within their history the Story of stories. In that discovery, the people recognized that the Pursuer had a Name, as Author of their narrative. For self and God alike, one's "identity seems largely determined by the kind of story which [one] understands [one's self] to have been enacting through the events of [one's] career, the story of [one's] life."[9]

5. *Entering One's Shadow*

The Myers-Briggs Type Indicator is a helpful contemporary tool for use in several spirit modes. It is based on the Jungian scales of Extroversion-Introversion (E-I), Judging-Perceiving (J-P), Thinking-Feeling (T-F), Intuitive-Sensing (N-S). One tends to have a predominance in each of these scales. The reader is referred to the material available for using this tool.[10] It is valuable here for several reasons. The first scale (E-I) indicates whether the God who is pursuing is most likely to be recognized externally or internally. The second scale (J-P) indicates whether, in approaching spiritual discipline, one is more likely to benefit from considering all the options carefully before deciding, or by following one's first inclination and plunge into practicing it. A pole in one of the two remaining scales (T-F or N-S) will be one's primary mode of functioning. The other pole in that same scale functions as one's "shadow," for as the least developed, it identifies one's major weakness. It is where one is most likely to experience the work of the Pursuer as "nasty."

The remaining scale indicates one's second and third functional preferences. Together with the primary and shadow functions, they identify the order of one's four functional preferences. These, in turn, suggest the progression one's spiritual development is likely to take, hinting of the direction from which the haunting sounds of the Pursuer are likely to come.

In addition, the first scale (E-I) likely indicates the largest disjunction in the arenas of one's spiritual life. Thus, the introvert needs to be lured into exploring the spirit modes richly present in the world of persons and objects—as the Trinity of Manifestation. The extrovert, in turn, needs discipline in pursuing those modes characteristic of the internal depths of silence and solitude—as the Trinity of Essence. In each case, one learns where the voice of the Pursuer is hardest to hear, for it thunders in places that one is not inclined to go.

6. *Empty Prayer*

In response to those who do not know how to pray, Paul says that it is just as well, for technique can get in the way. The best prayer, he insists, is when the Spirit prays for us.

> The Spirit helps us in our weakness; for we do not know how to pray as we ought, but the Spirit . . . intercedes for us with sighs too deep for words. And [God] who searches the hearts . . . knows what is the mind of the Spirit. (Rom. 8:26–27)

Go where you can be alone. Rather than praying intentionally as in dialogue, or halting all activity of the mind as in contemplation, simply let go. Permit anything and everything to enter your mind, with no filters. By becoming a blank slate, strive for pure listening and seeing and feeling, interested only in what may be whispered or what pictures might emerge on consignment. Do not be alarmed. Wait it out, with the trust that the circus before you, if not of God, will have God as a star participant.

7. *Meditation*

Among the words and phrases that one might wish to consider as focus guides for this spirit type are these: homesickness, yearning, not-quiteness, guilt, wistfulness, regret, haunted, hound of heaven, shadow, nostalgia, longing, urge, pursuit, search, stalk, providence.

8. *Music*

Among works worth considering for this spirit mode are Dvořák's Slavonic Dance No. 10, Beethoven's Concerto in D for Violin and Orchestra (second movement) and his Quartet No. 15 (third movement), and Mahler's Symphony No. 1 (first movement).

9. *Painting*

Over much of El Greco's work falls a shadow, leaving figures and landscapes in, but not ultimately of, this earth.[11] Nature and persons alike appear as strangers being lured back to their own element, going home to a place they have never been before. They appear as candlelike flickers, yearning and soaring and reaching as twisted gyrations of flesh claimed by a pursuing transcendence (for example, *Crucifixion* and *Opening of the Seventh Seal*).

Interestingly, one age of painting was particularly touched by this spirit type—the Renaissance. Leonardo da Vinci is a genius in capturing beauty born of wistful longing. In most of his faces appears a profound sadness, born in realizing the native limits of the possible. Whatever the subject, one finds in his work an ache of soul, incapable of finding peace within the limits of finitude alone (for example, *The Virgin and Child with St. Anne and John the Baptist*). What Berdyaev once mused about Botticelli's work could characterize the whole period: his Venuses yearn for earth, his Madonnas for heaven.

Remember that our purpose in suggesting paintings is not so much to understand them, as to find one on which to meditate, as "entry" into a particular spirit type.

A Summary

This spirit mode is slung between the titles of two Thomas Wolfe novels: *Look Homeward, Angel* and *You Can't Go Home Again*. Franz Kafka writes within this type, as if using a frazzled paintbrush. Everything once thought normal loses clear outline. In his *The Trial*, "K" is arrested on his thirtieth birthday, as the question "Why?" is thrust into his daily life. Thereupon pursued, his normal routine becomes a shambles—for the response, "Why not?" is no longer an answer. With similar eyes, T. S. Eliot watches the masses flow over London Bridge every morning on their way to work, returning each evening in order to make a peanut-butter-and-jelly sandwich with which to trudge back over the bridge in the morning, in order to . . . again and again. "I had not known death had undone so many."[12] This spirit mode begins when one of the pursued masses awakens, and in recognizing such life as death, becomes one of the few.

As a teacher, the path into this spirit mode gives me nightmares. Is it better for a student to be awakened, even if bereft of answers, than to continue unknowing as a sleepwalker among the living dead? One justification for pursuing people with questions rests in the belief that the living dead are haunted too. Either way, the effort to live without God entails living with the gnawing of one's unrecognized self. The hope on which this spirit mode rests is that through such relentlessness, one may recognize the name of the One who empties in order to fill. That name is Pursuer.

9

Promise and Delight
as New Innocence

Type 7: Play

As we begin to touch on the doings of God as Sanctifier, there is a sense of being "on the other side," of having passed through the darkness into a spirituality of promise. While one is never permitted to remain there exclusively, as in any of the modes, it is an important place to be. To be created and redeemed are experienced as an invitation into consummation. In the depth of all that is comes a promised radiance—of creative delight (type 7), of sacramental intent (type 8), and of call to completion (type 9). Each bequeaths a specialness to everything—to each sparrow, to every lily, and to each one of us.

The Other Side with Flourish

The identifying feature of this seventh mode as delight is "play." It evokes a sensitivity to the royal character of each speck of creation, hinting of its destiny as adopted. Here one is claimed by the intrinsic value of all things, simply in their existing, delightfully celebrated under a canopy of promise. One senses this in the delight of a wood-carver over the grain of a fine piece of oak. One senses this in the cherished specialness belonging to a child's cigar-box treasures—a shiny rock, a turtle shell, a special piece of ribbon. For eyes disciplined to see, such translucence extends to the birds of the air and the grass of the field, beheld as having a splendor belonging to things most precious.

I am writing this paragraph on a May morning. Of all possible scenarios, the Creator is sanctifying this day as one of a kind. What a glorious choice! With flamboyant dash, the warm breeze beckoning through the open window is God's invitation as playful lover. This is the One who, bringing joy to ear and eye, is "linking sense to sound and sight." To romp in any meadow today would mean being rebaptized into this spirit type given to each of us as a birth certificate. The child within becomes prematurely gray without a little child to lead. Strangely, the ID to be checked at the door of this spirit type is not to prove one's age, but one's youth. But how do we prove that we have become like children? A telltale sign is a lively curiosity in which every part of the world stands impatiently in line for special attention. The child within is awakened when the call to play establishes a rival priority for one's meals, work, and sleep.

But such exuberance is fragile. Early in my life it was bruised with the words "Empty out those pockets, throw away the junk in your room, and find something useful to do!" Childhood is an endangered species. Parental acceptance often requires that it be forfeited for instant adulthood, bringing "death" at an early age.

Sacred Secularity

This spirit mode has a capacity for reclaiming much that has been relinquished by tradition to the "secular." Printed on its label are these instructions: "Taste deeply of everything. Recognize yourself as wrapped in sound, fondled by textures, and invaded with smells. Let yourself be teased by the innuendo of each thing. Recognize, here, that 'more is better'!"

Lilt, joy, freshness—beginnings without end. Yes. Innocence, simplicity, gaiety, coolness, lightness, robustness, novelty. Yes, yes. Refreshing, dawning, blossoming, overflowing, radiant, serene, wholesome, youthful—childlike. Yes, yes, yes. The color is green, the time is now, and the goal is delight, for its own dear sake. The prayer is that each of us, if only for one reckless moment, may be extravagantly uncalculating. Taking no thought of the morrow, today becomes stuffed delightfully full of moments sufficient unto themselves.

Revealingly, Thomas Merton's deep-rootedness in the mystic spirituality of type 1 became deepened in time through hermit life in the desert (type 4), until he finally emerged into type 7. An important spiritual instrument for this pilgrimage was a camera. In his pictures is observable a growing fascination with the common as uncommon. With tender delight, he photographed the weathered grain of wood, the texture of moss, the surface of a worn and rusted pail—each with its own rare beauty, waving for attention at his lens.

God as Playmate

Scripture declares that we are fashioned in the image of God. By focusing on this triune God as Creator, we become valued as makers (*Homo faber*). When our focus shifts to God as Redeemer, we are illuminated in terms of wisdom—thus our scientific name (*Homo sapiens*). And with God recognized as Sanctifier, our nature becomes illuminated in terms of play (*Homo ludens*). Plato wisely insisted that "God alone is worthy of supreme seriousness." Thus our role is as "God's plaything, and that is the best part of [us]." For the Christian, this life of play is not one of solitaire, either for God or for us. The Divine-human relation here takes on an aura unique to playmates.

Scripture grounds this understanding by declaring that the foundations of the earth were marked out when God cavorted with Wisdom:

> "I was daily [God's] delight,
>   rejoicing before [God] always,
>   rejoicing in [God's] inhabited world
>   and delighting in [its children]."
> (Prov. 8:30–31)

Huizinga's brilliant study of play rests on a powerful conclusion: that one enters the "circle of play by turning toward the ultimate."[1] The reverse is equally true.

Spiritual Laughter

This spirit type builds on insights from other modes. Its roots are nurtured by the knowledge that no matter how profound one's acts may be, something problematic will always remain. Monarchs who fail to acknowledge this cannot laugh at themselves, and thus their doings become lethal, no matter how benevolent the intent. Play is the neutralizer of our bravado. Thus those deprived of a special affection for Mickey Mouse are not fit for God's realm.

Some years ago, I was drinking coffee with one of my colleagues from the history department at Princeton. The United States Presidential election had just been won by the largest electoral vote in history. "You just watch," he said. "This country is in trouble. That man has no sense of humor—especially about himself." "That man's" name was Richard Nixon.

Childlikeness

Painters who operate within this spirit type seem restricted by modern culture to find inspiration within their own subjectivity. One might conclude that only the interior lodgings of imagination and memory seem left to save the poet-soul from extinction. Relatedly, today's utilitarian world offers few playthings fit for nurturing a free and grinning spirit.

Thus, if famished from without, this spirit mode requires a rebirth from within. One's membership card needs to be stamped: "Childlike." But how? I do not know how the disciples felt when Jesus set before them a little child. I know how I feel. It makes me sad. Rebirth means remembering with awe what it was like to have once had this spirit that birth so lavishly bestowed on it. The "fall" is a name for the fact that childlikeness is so rare in adults.

In spite of popular opinion, this loss comes not from a natural entropy of the human spirit grown weary by the long haul. In truth, imagination is systematically rooted out, for a profit. A stuffed sock is no match for a Barbie doll, and scraps of cloth, assembled with imagination, rarely survive intimidation by her ready-made cocktail outfit with high heels. Gone is the sheer joy of running barefoot in the grass, rendered obsolete by the compulsion to have hundred-dollar jogging shoes. Games now require packaged sets and special equipment, for a piece of chalk and a slab of sidewalk cannot be retailed. So it is that as adults we come to prefer watching professionals "play," for a price, rather than playing ourselves, for free. Over the whole falls a shadow. A spirit of competitive seriousness turns play into games, and games into deadly contests.

The Promising and Make-Believe

This posture of childlikeness may best be grasped through its opposite. Dullness is the name for life without promise, when things simply are what they are, and never more. By contrast, the artist's eyes ignite things with radiant possibility, so that things are what they have about them *to be,* and never less. Such joy is present simply in the seeing, even if none of the possibilities are ever attempted. So this spirit type resides not in the promise *of* something, but in something's *being* promising—in the intensity of its own radiant concreteness.

With such eyes the psalmist beholds "all the earth" breaking forth in "joyful noise" as "a new song." The sound of this music is a thundering of the sea, as in accompaniment

> "the rivers clap their hands
> and the hills ring out their joy"
> (Ps. 97:8, Paulist [Hebrew, 98:8]).

Without purpose, reward, or advantage, the universe sings to its own dance—on and on, utterly and totally and completely for its own sake, even if we fail to participate.

An image that emerges from this spirit mode is that of God as the child artist at play. Ecstatically smeared from head to toe, God paints nothingness into being with gaudy abandonment, deliriously in love with creating for its own sake. When looking at the artwork of a child, we are told, do not ask, "What is it?" Instead, say, "Tell me about it." So with God. And in such telling, one comes to understand Saint Thérèse of Lisieux's insistence on being a plaything for God. By playing together, she confessed, "I want the Child Jesus to be so happy in my heart that He won't think of going back to heaven."[2]

Although "make-believe" can be escape, it can also entail the courage to dream in the face of life's daily patterns of boredom and/or oppression. Just as type 1 is a spirituality purified of all doing, type 7 is a spirituality purified of all utility. Its value is intrinsic, for its own delightful sake. That is what characterizes play as play. It is what can transform any activity into play.

Innocence

A distinctive gift of Christianity to the modern world could be its vindication of the eyes of the child. Life beheld with the anticipatory "magic" too often reserved for Christmas Eve renders the lowly corners aglow with new birth, while Magi bring forth gifts from the far country as the skies overhead become rumored with the sound of angels. Isaiah's dream is of an ongoing Christmas Eve, where none shall "hurt or destroy" for "a little child shall lead them" (Isa. 11:6, 9). Jesus, too, is clear about who can see the new heaven and the new earth. And so let us repeat, lest we missed it the first time: "And calling to him a child, he put him in

the midst of them, and said, 'Truly, I say to you, unless you turn
and become like children, you will never enter the kingdom"
(Matt. 18:2–3).

Such spirituality is not to be confused with shallow silliness, or
with the temptation to mischief after two drinks at "happy hour."
Sanctification as delight comes "after" redemption. This means
that our play is most to be trusted when the balloons of our self-
importance have undergone several rounds of puncturing. A favorite sin is to take ourselves with a seriousness deserving only of
God. Laughter breaks such seriousness into a re-creation of that
foolish innocence by which play is blessed.

Such childlikeness brings new eyes to the "practice" of religion. Above all, liturgy takes on the purity of distilled play. Thus,
the priest who frowns on chewing bubble gum in the sacristy is in
danger of turning precious playing into the tedium of dutiful
work. The fundamental question God may someday address to
both nations and individuals may well be this: "How well have
you learned to play together?"

EXERCISES

1. *The Sabbath as Play*

We live in a culture where "demythologizing" is often claimed
as the best way to gain a hearing for religion. Spirit type 7, however, insists on the contrary. Christianity is best understood by
not reducing it to verifiable concepts. Christianity is an invitation
to mythologize, to dream and imagine and play life into reality.
For some of us, this requires the company of a child as permission
to enter. Borrow one for the day and head for the zoo. The giraffe
has to be one of God's better jokes. But if you insist on beginning
as a spectator, watch persons sand-castling on Sunday afternoons
at the beach. Or, in the Plains states, look for kites and hot-air
balloons. I have even caught glimpses of it among Eastern sophis-
ticates, walking barefoot in Central Park.

Walt Disney has marketed this mode with irresistible sentimentality. From the animations and fantasies he began have
sprung worlds where crickets become consciences, elephants fly,
and wicked witches get what is coming to them. This mode relates
to that yearly ritual of tears in which we watch Judy Garland as she
pleads to fly over the rainbow. It is experienced as the urge to give

names of endearment to cars, to talk to animals, and never to throw away velveteen rabbits. It is reborn when one recalls, without a touch of embarrassment, the name of one's first teddy bear. Its birthday is Christmas Eve, when yearly one relearns that joy is in the anticipation more than the arrival.

These are the times in which faith is identified not as certainty about what is, but as "the assurance of things hoped for, the conviction of things not seen" (Heb. 11:1). In this spirit type we are invited to know ourselves as the ones blessed by "sojourn[ing] in the land of promise" (Heb. 11:9). In the philistine world of utility in which one and one always equal only two, the ones and the twos become fatally withered.

The truth of all this is contained in one word— "Sabbath."[3] This means taking time to live now in the promise. Scripture is clear about its centrality. On the seventh day even God rested. Yet I grew up dreading Sunday. It was the day in which everything was forbidden, when Mother could not even cook, and Dad refused to buy a newspaper, certainly not one with comics. My faith took a fatal plunge on the morning the preacher suggested that heaven will be a perpetual Sunday.

It has taken me forty years to understand that "Sabbath refraining" is supposed to have a positive intent. Refraining from work is to guarantee time and space for play. The Sabbath is the day for wearing red socks—and matching suspenders. The God who hand-dipped each star in glitter and personally taught the dolphins their breast stroke insisted on having time to enjoy it all. Spirituality insists on such periods of doing nothing and feeling no guilt.

Yet in a culture ruled by the Protestant work ethic there is little hope for the rebirth of such a spirit type—unless, ironically, one is *forced* to take time off weekly for holy leisure. Some may prefer a Saturday night when, dressed garishly after an afternoon's rummaging in used-clothes stores, one goes out on the town to make believe. For the more inhibited, an unpretentious start might be a half hour of nursery rhymes read aloud, or TV with the sound turned off, or an Easter hymn sung to the tune of a Christmas carol. At the very least, read again *The Little Prince*, or resample Dr. Seuss. Are you blessed enough still to have any of your childhood books? Remember Nancy Drew, the Hardy Boys, Dave Dawson, or even Tom Swift?

A Sabbath is likewise a vintage time for exploring a new town or a strange part of one's own city. It is an invitation to discover ethnic neighborhoods, to taste new things, and to find places where one can be sufficiently "invisible" to risk unusual behaviors. Short of that, anyone for Parcheesi?

My children were my permission to play. When they left home, my spirit was in jeopardy. As my last daughter was about to enter the bus on her way to college, she drew me aside. "Never let me grow up," she pleaded. I promised, if the vow could be mutual. One week later, a package arrived. Inside was a well-known figure for my pocket, with the words "Never let the Mickey Mouse in your soul die."

Clowning is an internal Sabbath. If you are timid, begin by yourself, and only later clown with a friend. Others do better by beginning with a person with whom they are inclined normally "to clown." In either case, get some face paint, a clay nose or two, two or three rubber ears, some clothing that is both colorful and too big. Discover for yourself a persona by playing unhurriedly with lots of paint and one face. More times than not, one unknowingly paints one's Sabbath face, the one yearning to get out from behind the workaday mask. Practice letting it grin back at you from a mirror. Another experiment is for two persons to give each other personas, each making explicit the one discerned as waiting patiently inside one's friend.

Painted faces give permission to enter a silent world where one no longer has to explain oneself. It is amazing, once one moves beyond the initial inhibition, how free one feels. The gift is an unexpected security, where one is vulnerable but protected, real yet theatrical, honest while pretending. Ironically, a "false face" permits one to risk hiding no longer.

2. *Lectio Divina*

On a related but contrasting note, the church has held in high regard the practice of *lectio divina*, or sacred reading. It used to be common for part of each Sabbath to be used in this way, for hearing the scriptural promise made concrete. This practice has been largely replaced by Bible study. The latter is concerned to learn scriptural sources, background, and specific contexts, in an effort to decipher what the writers were doing in their day. *Lectio*, however, is quite different. It means reading scripture with the expectation of being addressed by God now. The purpose is not to seek but to be sought. Thus our Puritan ancestors read the scriptures as if they were a collection of personal letters from God. My hermit friend put it well: "I have learned to read scripture as if my name is Israel."

Meditation has long had the meaning of tasting with the lips. Therefore "an early metaphor used to describe *lectio* is that of eating. A morsel of food is taken, chewed over, broken apart, and swallowed. *Lectio divina* is like that."[4] This technique is particularly true of scripture, for since it is intended to be proclaimed, it is meant to be heard, more than seen—physically, with mouth and ears. Thus, for much of church history the word meditation itself meant reading scripture to one's own self aloud. The purpose was to savor each word and phrase for its own sake, much as one feels when hearing a poet read her own poetry. One rolls words around on the tongue, plays with inflection, samples meaning, adjusts the volume, and fiddles with the tone controls. In a word, the self learns to "play" with scripture.

For recapturing one approach to this discipline, take a familiar passage of scripture, such as the Twenty-third Psalm or a lectionary reading for the day.[5] Read it through slowly, thoughtfully, aloud. Do it a second time, even slower, savoring the parts. Then center in on a sentence by which one is particularly struck. Taste each word in turn, such as in this example:

"*The* Lord is my shepherd."
"The *Lord* is my shepherd."
"The Lord *is* my shepherd."
"The Lord is *my* shepherd."
"The Lord is my *shepherd*."

Then permit one word or phrase to surface. Keep it, cherish it, play with it, repeat it, as God's word of promise to you this day.

3. Newspaper Prayer

In a "secular" variation of *lectio*, take a section of the newspaper, any section. Tear it in half, top to bottom, then side to side. Shuffle the pieces, and take one. Read it, expecting to be addressed. Even the section composed of ads, classified or commercial, can prove fertile. Try the experiment several times.

4. Creativity

An important exercise in exorcizing the adult world threatening access to this spirit type is to permit the artist inside each of us to bubble forth, if only for a short time. Take anything in sight— papers, pencils, any available objects. Make candy-corn designs on a table, construct a cushion house, squeeze toothpaste pictures on a window, carve a soap pig, fasten toothpicks together with play dough to form a tower, use pliers to make a paper clip zoo. Let these objects find their rightful relationships. Stay out of their way, content to be their playmate. Was I the only child in captivity who liked to build pyramids out of canned goods?

For those who need "forced feeding," buy a coloring book. For the first time in your life, deliberately color *outside the lines*. Remember that life refuses to stay within neat borders. Let yourself cherish the world of purple cows. Be sure to smell the color of each crayon. Recall when recess was your favorite subject.

I knew that a friend's spiritual conversion was for real when he began building model airplanes again, and taught his business partners how to play jacks during coffee break. These are the outer marks of innocence restored. Buy yourself a teddy bear, as an offspring of the one you are ready to remember.

Visit the children's section of the public library. Check out several books. If the librarian is uneasy, offer to leave pictures of your grandchildren as collateral. Ask permission to attend the weekday or Saturday morning story hour. Bring your teddy bear.

5. *Silent Meal*

Largely lost is the experience of eating as a delight. Most of us take our meals on the run, or in excess, or both. Even when a meal becomes more intentional, conversation tends to become the focus. As an exercise, set aside time for a silent meal, eating either by yourself or with others. Eat deliberately, bite by bite, sip by sip. Experience the difference between delight in eating anything, and this exercise of taking delight in the eating of each thing in particular. Let each food be what it is, uniquely so, and delight in it. Give yourself to the buttered corn, the cold milk, the yellow peach. Taste the breadiness of bread, the "mashiness" of potatoes. Be direct in experiencing the flavors, the crunch, the colors, the aromas, the tanginess—and the chewing, the swallowing, the sensation of sufficient fullness. Surround the whole event in the wrappings of thanksgiving.

6. *The Charismatic Sensitivity*

The book of Acts indicates how widespread a practice it was in the early church to be baptized in the Spirit. One became so swept by the Abyss as Spirit that one began "speaking in tongues." While in type 1, one reenters God as Abyss, here the Abyss enters us as Sanctifier.

For this, one can do no more than ask, and prepare. Such an experience need be neither bizarre nor uncommon. An analogy is teenagers lost in the frenzy of dancing, much as Native Americans become in their own sacred ceremonies. The clue is to relinquish control, becoming moved by emotion. As a beginning, assume the posture of request, with palms outstretched and open. Then raise your arms with fingers open, moving, fluttering. Reach for all that you ever yearned for, stretching upward on extended tiptoes. Do it again, and again. Music, such as a recording of Native American music, is helpful. Make comparable sounds. Sway with the beat. Let your feet move. Step to the beat, each time with knees slightly higher, until you become the beat. It will be sufficient unto itself.[6]

7. *Meditation*

Words that this mode might suggest for meditation include promise, innocence, trust, whimsy, delight, beginnings, mischief, novelty, radiance, humor, pleading, fun, lure, enchantment, mellowness, intensity, freshness, glint—and Mickey Mouse.

As an additional exercise, choose one word that seems particularly appropriate. Then consult a thesaurus, tasting slowly each word suggested as synonym and antonym.

8. *Poetry*

Type 7 is intent on a world furnished freely and luxuriously as if by a lyric poet. It is the earth bathed in promise. Find a book of good lyric poetry. May I suggest e. e. cummings? Read some of the poems aloud. Push delight toward the edge, where it waves at silliness. Give in to it by trying Vachel Lindsay or Ogden Nash. Then try writing poetry yourself, putting words together in the most outlandish and unlikely combinations. Don't write a poem—become one, in your own unique gibberish. Let yourself frolic in the thick, moist lushness of metaphor and imagery. Something deep dies if one asks, "What good does that do?"

9. *Painting*

To see the world through the yes of this spirit mode, one can be aided by the paintings of Klee.[7] His is the world of whimsy—childlike, playful fantasy, wherein the doodling dream state of the ordinary takes on an uncanny energy, hinting of spirit. His brush is like an introspective memory, with a knack for daubing with nostalgia whatever it touches. It is a restored world, where child-like innocence makes miracles at home. His paintings are invitations to unbridle imagination, so that the thoughts of the cosmos seem to think themselves, without need to think (for example, *The Dancer*). Even in the sadness of Klee's later years, dream shapes along the tragic frontiers still ventured into fantasy as promise (as, for example, *Portrait of Gaia*).

10. *Music*

One musician who was not inhibited about bringing playful humor into and around his music was Franz Joseph Haydn. Taste some of this in his *Toy* Symphony, *Surprise* Symphony, and *Farewell* Symphony. On a delightful note, consider Grétry's *Danses Villageoises*, Offenbach's *Gaité Parisienne*, and "Farewell" from Schubert's *Swan Songs*.

A Summary

Too often Providence is understood as a preset plan. Thus God's "will" takes on the power of law, with the only choice being either to do it or be punished. In this spirit type, however, Providence is no longer seen through the eyes of the juror, but through those of the artist. It is experienced not as Divine manipulation, but as shimmering promise, hinted at in all that is, as new beauty at unborn depth. Providence begins as the lure of surface is made deep by Divine promise. What something is, is what it has about it to be.

In type 8, to which we now turn, such sanctification grasps us as symbolic meaning. In type 9, we will explore sanctification as the call to transfigured doing. But in the type we are summarizing, sanctification is experienced as delight in things for their own sake, enjoyed simply in being beheld with the eyes of promise. This is not a promise *that*, but a promise *of*.

10

The Secular
as Daily Sacrament

Type 8: Things

This spirit mode is a variation on the theme of concrete life as sanctified, applying and expanding the meaning of Incarnation (type 5). But things here are not grasped in intrinsic delight, as we just explored in type 7, nor are we called to be midwives, as in our final spirituality (type 9). Here things encounter us with sacramental power.

The I-Thou Relationship

There is an important distinction between transparency and incarnation. Transparency entails the sacrifice of particularity. In the act of being emptied, persons and objects can point beyond themselves, evoking experiences of the Ground of Being. The more transparent something becomes, the more perfectly does it stand for that which it is not. In that sense, using Tillich's images, the concrete is "crucified" so that it becomes "resurrected" as symbol for the power of being. This transparency is what we experienced in the first three spirit types — through mystery, order, and dynamism. Thus, for instance, one is claimed not by the mystery *of* a starry night, but by Mystery Itself, evoked *by* a star-drenched sky. Through loss of particularity, symbolic power draws one into undifferentiated unity.

Incarnation is different, as illuminated by a crisis in the life of Martin Buber. After Buber had a conversation with a student, that person went and committed suicide. In lamenting over his possible implication in that death, Buber was pushed to distinguish two types of relation. In transparency, something becomes a means, rather than an end. This, Buber pondered, could have been the case with the student—feeling reduced to an object. Thus he sensed the need for another type of relation, in which something is experienced as an end. One is regarded not transparently, as if a conduit to "otherness," but incarnationally, as a rightful resident.

In spirit type 8, then, involvement comes not through absorption but through what Buber calls an I-Thou relationship. Here one greets and is greeted, by anything—from a tree to a person.[1] Such sacramental reciprocity is the mutual address of subject to subject. All things can be encountered as Thous, acknowledging all of life as sacred. Such mutuality stands in contrast to "I-It" relations, constituted by an objective stand of subject observing object, reducing "otherness" to being *only* a thing.

This spiritual disposition makes contact with what W. H. Auden calls contemplation. As he uses the term, it is the discipline of making one's full self totally available to another, in an act of pure immediacy. Such an interactive relation is a necessity, he insists, for all persons in each department of every university. Mutuality is imperative, whether one is peering microscopically at a biological mystery, being part of the emerging rhythmic pattern of a musical composition, or learning therapy as discernment of connections within a patient's unsuspected coherence. In each, concreteness dare not be forfeited. It must be encountered as an intense distillation of presence. Such presence, in turn, is knowable only through the discipline of focused self-availability. It is then that "otherness" becomes immediacy, as I is to Thou.

The Sacramental

Expressed in traditional Christian terminology, this mode is concerned with the sacramental capacity of all that exists. In the history of religions, there has hardly been any material or object which, at some time or another, has not been regarded sacramentally—from water to hair to salt. But what can the sacramental come to mean in today's secularized world, without resorting to some sort of quasi magic? *Sacramentality would mean encountering each concreteness as if experiencing it for the first time.*

Expressed another way, it would entail seeing and hearing and touching and smelling and tasting *incarnationally*. At its intimate heart, this mode involves greeting each person as the presence of a sacramental gift, inviting a relationship sacredly unlike any other. Such specialness Jesus roots in God's knowing each sparrow by name and numbering our wayward hairs before one of them can reach the bathroom floor.

Each as First

Developing this spirit mode as a disciplined attitude might be difficult. Sensing what it would be like to do so, however, is not. It requires remembering one's first drink of icy water from a sparkling mountain stream. With that image center stage, imagine taking a sip, wiping your lips with your sleeve, and with a huge smile handing the cup to your friend with the words, "The blood of Christ!" Equally sacramental, for me, is the first cup of coffee in the morning.

How early in life does a sense for this dimension occur? One of my first memories of it was as a child, smelling bacon cooking as I snuggled in my sleeping bag. Once begun, images tumble forth. There is the first mockingbird in spring, the fall sun filtered by painted leaves, a full moon over city lights on a night flight, an unknown child's sly smile on a Bangkok street, a deer clearing a meadow fence on an April morning. Each is a delight, as we sensed in type 7. But here our search is for something else—not delightful surface, but sacramental depth. Each "now" is like a special beholding of the morning star on the first morning of creation, as it dances its response to God's invitation for there to be light. And we are there.

Separateness as Fall

Tillich was asked once what he meant by "the fall." His response came quickly: the fact that there is an altar as well as one's desk, that one's daily meals are not the Lord's Supper. The intent of the spirit mode we are exploring is to reclaim such sacramental interconnectedness. Then it is that one's morning shower becomes an ongoing baptism, one's dwelling a domestic church, grace before each meal a eucharistic prayer, each vocation a calling, and every new beginning a miracle.

Cultivating such a sacramental sensitivity begins with the discipline of focused immediacy. Eyes, cleansed and freshened by dropping "the scales of inattention," sense in the commonplace a "brilliant identity, a luminous quality," a sacramental "firstness." Then it is that "things seem to have more 'suchness': red is redder, water is wetter, and mud is muddier."[2] So engaged with "suchness," as if by a Thou, Presence speaks to presence.

The Shroud of Forgetting

If this mode is as available as one's nearest coffee cup, why is it so little experienced, or at least acknowledged? The "fall" as shadow is a variation of the universal sin we perceived elsewhere—of taking things for granted. The pattern of Israel's history is a paradigm for spirit life. Israel's repetitive rhythm is one of growing affluence and power, accompanied by forgetfulness, followed by judgment as sterile emptiness, resulting in reversal as rebirth. So it is for each of us, and for our times, over and over again. *More is never enough, nor will it ever be.* This one fact, seemingly so simple to remember, becomes massive in consequence when forgotten. But to remember it is to be blessed, by the little in which there is depth sufficient to overflowing. Here again, the threat of nothingness is what can shake a person into focused immediacy. When all that is for sure is the thin slice of nowness immediately before me, that intensity becomes sacramental, as the pearl of great price.

The Last as Beginning Again

An illustration may be helpful. Imagine yourself condemned to die on death row. Count with growing dread the few days remaining. One by one they pass, too quickly, until on the final night one hears the question: "What would you like for your last meal?" An incredible question, designed to tear at the fabric of even the most languid. "Roast beef, medium rare!" You count the bites, down to the last. The very last! Never again. Then the walk, until there are four steps. Then three. Now two. Only one! Never again. Seated on one's last chair. Cold. Straps. Clammy. Counting the breaths. Down to the final three. Never again, *ever*! As your eyes involuntarily flinch at "one," the phone rings. The governor. "Let him go!"

What would you say then? "Thanks, but let me think about this"? Indeed! As for me, there would be no small steps aimed toward that exit. It would be leaps. Out through the main door. Down the front steps, four at a time, and counting. A huge smile to the guard in the tower, with a wave to his equally huge machine gun. Somersaults, barefoot in the grass, dandelions behind each ear. Never would sky be skyier, nor grass grassier. Straight to Mc-

Donald's, for the biggest orange juice ever poured. "The blood of Christ!" Looking deeply into the eyes of the clerk would be like seeing deep brown for the first time. Would she understand, as she glances at the clock in the hope that less and less time is left? How could she? But for one whose time has come dangerously close to nothing, then it is that *anything* feels like everything.

To live each day as if the last is to live exponentially the first day of the rest of one's life. That is to live sacramentally. It is understandable, then, that it was while in exile that John could write the book of Revelation, singing of the universe as a jeweled tabernacle of the Holy of holies, each object a chalice. "Take this, all of you, and drink from it."

This spirit mode renders life a daily sacrament, as long as one remembers that each of everything could be the last. If forgotten, this sacramentalism of ongoing "firstness" corrodes into the blabby boredom of weary repetition:

> All things are full of weariness;
> a [person] cannot utter it;
> the eye is not satisfied with seeing,
> nor the ear filled with hearing.
> What has been is what will be,
> and what has been done is what will be done;
> and there is nothing new under the sun.
>
> (Eccl. 1:8–9)

Eucharist as Gratitude

Sacraments are so essential to Christianity that a worship service composed only of talk borders on self-contradiction. With Incarnation at its heart, talking *about* the gospel is no substitute for participation from *within*. In a majority of scriptural accounts, the resurrection is portrayed as Presence experienced through the breaking of bread (for example, Luke 24:13–35). Pentecost, in turn, is confirmation that the God who was Incarnate as flesh continues as Spirit to be available as incarnational Presence everywhere (Acts 2:1–21). Thus Eucharist, or Holy Communion, is at the heart of Christian experience. While explanations of "how" vary widely, there is a remarkable consensus that the heart of Eucharistic experience is "Real Presence." Calvin says it as well as any. God is present in, with, under, by, and through the common-day elements. Once experienced there, it is understandable that St. Augustine recognized not simply two or even seven sacraments. The places at which the Spirit sanctifies us through things, he insists, are innumerable.

EXERCISES

1. *Sacramentals*

The church has come to distinguish a "sacrament" from a "sacramental." A sacrament is an intersection of action and material through which God has promised to act in a way that would not otherwise be so. For the Protestant, such uniqueness is reserved for two sacraments—Baptism and Eucharist, as uniquely instituted by Jesus. Roman Catholics recognize seven, providing Divine empowerment at the hinge points of life—birth (baptism), coming of age (confirmation), nurture (eucharist), sexuality (marriage), vocation (ordination), sin (confession), sickness and death (anointing/viaticum).

Sacramentals, on the other hand, are acts or objects that evoke awareness of what is already so, independent of the sacramentals themselves. Their task is evocation, recalling what is important but so often forgotten. Thus, for example, recalling what is important but so often forgotten. Thus, for example, the sacrament of Baptism effects, once and for all, one's incorporation into the body of Christ. Holy water, on the other hand, is a sacramental, reminding us that this is so.

Protestants tend to be suspicious of sacramentals, quick to point out their magical or idolatrous misuse. No doubt there will always be some persons who light votive candles to guarantee success, or use holy water to remove corns. A Protestant friend snorted loudly at a recent basketball game when a Catholic player crossed himself before attempting a free throw that would determine the game. His disdain would be valid if the player's intent was to gain help after the ball left his hands. That would be magic, not a sacramental. It was a sacramental, however, if the player's intent was to keep things in perspective by remembering: "If we win, we win to the Lord; if we lose, we lose to the lord; so whether we win or whether we lose, we are the Lord's" (see Rom. 14:7–9).

In truth, no one is without sacramentals. Protestant pastors will experience this quickly if they remove the American flag from the chancel, or neglect to print a bulletin, or shift the location of the Communion table, or put the basketball trophies in storage, or replace the cross with one more to their liking, or even borrow a coffeepot from the church kitchen without proper permission. The issue is not sacramentals or no sacramentals. The issue is to determine which sacramentals are idolatrous and which are evocative of a genuine I-Thou relation.

Sorting out the possessions of a dead loved one is a process of discerning those personal items which are inviolable—a favorite pen, coffee mug, comb, watch, ring. In such moments, one is in the presence of personal sacramentals. To discard them is a sacrilege, and to give them to strangers borders on violation. They can be given only to those who will recognize them for the sacramentals they are. Now try to identify some, especially your own:

- As an experiment, identify ten possessions which your friends would be inclined to identify as sacramentals at your death. Rank them in importance. Focus on why they so function.
- If one's pocketbook or wallet is stolen, one is likely to post this notice: "Keep the money, but please return the other things. They have only sentimental value." The right word is "sacramental." Take your pocketbook or wallet and empty it. Sort what you find into three piles: what is useful, what should be discarded, and all the rest. Reflect on "all the rest." What makes them sacramentals?
- Do the same with your glove compartment or your car trunk. Or schedule with family or friends a sacramental cleaning of the attic. In discovering forgotten "treasures" one can sense how Israel's understanding of religion as storytelling creates sacramentals. At Passover, the youngest child asks, "Why do we do these things?" In the attic, the ongoing litany will be: "What on earth is this thing?" As stories of remembrance are told, special will be the words of blessing: "Let's keep it."
- Visit grandparents or older friends. Ask them to tell you about their "prized possessions." Remind them of old trunks, and make overtures about photograph albums. Such bonding through sharing is what scripture identifies as covenant.
- Visit a nursing home. If you can become sufficiently trusted, a resident may share the contents of the "cigar box" in her night stand. During such a sacred event, two ticket stubs, several poems, and a lock of hair will take on the power of "thou"-ness.
- Invite someone to be with you (preferably a child) as you sort through the clothes in your closet. Discern which should be

kept and what may be given an exit visa.
- Do an inventory of your home. If robbed, which things would be "irreplaceable"? A sacramental is most inclined to occur in the space opened up by such a question.
- If you were to move overseas, with all your physical needs automatically met, what three things would you choose to take with you?
- Enter a particular room in your house. Carefully identify marks, dents, chips, smudges, flaws, colors. Deliberately let each tell its story.

Identify seven things that you tend to do every day. Choose one of these to be done each day of a week as a sacramental. As appropriate, be attentive to such matters as "vestment" to be worn, elements to be used, words to be said, and ambience to be created. For example, if one's choice is a bath, consider such sacramentals as candles, oil, amount of water, incense, color, temperature, and texture of towel.

For a trial period, make a disciplined use of some traditional sacramentals. For example, make the sign of the cross on yourself as reminder that you no longer own yourself; you have been bought with a price; you are "branded." Or genuflect in front of that which helps you acknowledge that you are not the center of your own world. Place a glass of water beside your front door. Place your finger in it as you come and go, recalling the liberation that comes in knowing that in baptism your death has already been died. Permit candles, bells, and incense to speak in their own gentle way.

A prayer over a meal is called "giving thanks" (*eucharistia*). Take a day in which to say such a blessing of thanksgiving over every meal, each snack, at the places of entrance and exit to your dwelling, in the center of its rooms for sleeping and eating, sharing and aloneness. Bless the special objects there, consecrating them to the task of rendering sacramental one's common acts. When ready, extend such blessings to your place of work — without getting holy water on the time sheets! Do the same for your modes of communication, and of transportation. The intent is to invite all of life to reveal itself as gifts upon Gift. Finally, do a blessing at those real or symbolic places of destruction in your community.

Sanctify a particular space with sacramentals witnessing to humankind's diverse spiritual perspectives as "family." Consider, for example, a Jewish prayer shawl, a rosary, a family Bible, a Buddhist meditation mat, a bowl of Navaho corn pollen, and a Greek Orthodox icon.

Create a sacred space that is an expansion of who you really are. Remember when you did this spontaneously as a child— in a tree house, a special place under the porch, a sacred tree. If you have forgotten, ask yourself where you went to cry, and where you did your dreaming. Furnish that space with sacramentals that lay claim to your identity. Take time to let them make their own requests for inclusion. May Sarton knew the power of sacramentals for sacralizing space. During bitter snowstorms she defiantly brought cut flowers into her home.

A Japanese tea ceremony is an act of gentle presence. Create your own with a friend, either yourself or someone else. It is a time for being graced by the simple ingredients and motions of integrity. Create a setting that is simple, modest, and gracious. Take off your shoes before entering, as if on holy ground. Sit on the floor or carpet, as symbol of direct contact with things. Let the atmosphere be one of quiet respect, treating all things with the care belonging to fine china. Be wholly present, hearing the water boiling, the sound of the pouring, the smile of waiting until things are "just so." Taste in gentle sips, with moments of quiet conversation made up of only a sentence or two by each person at a time. Permit listening to predominate, as symbol of being having precedent over doing. Let each gesture be taken only because it is needed, taking the time to form it graciously. Beauty emerges when every part is necessary, and each is a gesture of the whole. Use pottery, weaving, wood—the simple givens that gently push aside plastic soda, Styrofoam, and hurry. The spiritual blessing adorning such special times resides in simplicity as the timeless motion of gentle order. Hospitality rests in treating each person as the Divine incognito, expanded until everything is a guest.

In this modern consumptive culture, one is tempted to stereotype asceticism as primitive and ascetics as deprived. A visit to environments shaped by Shakers, Puritans, and Quakers prove otherwise. The word "ascetic" means one who is made lean with exercise until disciplined into freedom from self-indulgence. To be controlled from one's own center rather than from without is a noble trait. And what is wise for one's bodily stature needs to give shape to one's environment. For a beginning, take an hour in your home to simplify your environment. This usually means removing accumulated clutter. While one might guess that the result would feel empty, it usually takes on the power of gift. Remain within this space, and let its leaven work.

A gesture from Asian culture is significant. In the United States, we are unsure about how to greet one another. The sound written "Hi" is ambiguous, to say the least. Little better are the words "How are you?" when the only response considered courteous is "Fine." As an alternative, greet a friend with a gentle bow. This is to acknowledge the divine form of "Thouness" in all of life. If an explanation seems needed, simply say, "The Spirit in me greets the Spirit in you."

2. Feelings

While type 1 has as its objective to "turn off," the task of this mode is to "turn on." Yet today's bombardment of the senses, ironically, is such an overload that survival forces us to "tune things out." Mozart is reduced to elevator ambience, unheard radio chatter is filler for loneliness, and businesses fill telephone waiting with empty sound. Such dulling of the senses disconnects the self from its feelings, dissipating them into mindless ambience. Men tend to go a step farther, burying what is left under a macho mask of control and practicality. The poker-face disguise of nonfeeling "in-charge-ness" is groomed as a world-weary emblem of one who has seen it all. Instead of living as direct encounter, we become once removed from everything—watching our experience and thinking our feelings. So restricted, we are denied direct access even to the sacramental depth of our own selves.

Getting one's head out of the way of one's feelings requires asking oneself at inopportune moments, "What am I feeling *right now*?" Insist on direct feelings, without mediating images. "I think that I feel . . . " is no acceptable preface. One technique for doing this is so to associate several common-day acts with the question that it becomes raised automatically. For example, ask yourself every time you enter an elevator or turn the ignition key in your car. Make it the first thing to enter the mind upon rising, and the last to leave at night. Post the question on the bathroom mirror, or the refrigerator, or as a greeting inside the front door. Ask someone you see often to keep asking you that question.

Each of us has a primary sense. I had not known this until someone played an ambience tape of various sounds—rain on a roof, the crackle of fire, the deep breathing of excitement, the sound of a stream. Then I knew. Take time to test each of your senses. Touch different textures; go to a tea store and smell their offerings; try a winery for tasting; spend an afternoon at an art gallery; take a tape recorder and sample the sounds existing within a mile of your home. Once you have decided, favor your primary sense by giving it free play. Develop it into an art form.

As another exercise, deliberately cultivate the sense most unused. With intentionality, make it a point to "come to your senses."

Chanting is a phenomenon known in almost every culture. The one who chants a prayer, it is said, prays twice. Learn several versions of Gregorian chants for use with praying the psalms.[3] As a variation, create a chant of two lines. Begin a psalm on any note. End the last word of the line by going up one note. Begin the second line on that same note, and end the last word by going down one step to the original note. Repeat this pattern until the psalm is finished. Early monks memorized all 150 psalms so they could chant them by heart as they worked. Idle whistling is a modern equivalent. Try sacramentalizing your work by chanting, if only to yourself, using the Twenty-third Psalm or the Lord's Prayer.

In the privacy of your car, use the above chant technique and make up words, expressing your feelings about what is happening around you. God will appreciate it, even if it sounds no better than this: "O God, this is quite a morning/and that cow along the road looks silly,/but so am I making these noises,/yet it's good to be alive!"

3. Nowness

Few of us live much of our lives in immediacy. Since the present is an ever-moving line where past and future converge, our tendency is to live either in what was, or in anticipation of what might be. My parents were such products of the Great Depression that in remembering the past, their future was controlled by fear of what might be. I did not know the depression, but I learned quickly from them the power of the future to kidnap the present. I "couldn't wait" until I went to kindergarten. Once there, I couldn't wait until I could discard knickers for long pants. But that "arrival," in turn, was gobbled up by another "future." I yearned for when I would be able to drive. This, in turn, paled before the image of graduating from college, then getting my first job, receiving a promotion, having a family, building a dream house, seeing the kids safely grown up, retiring, in order to . . . *die!* For most of us, each present is either too soon or too late.

When my mother died, having "made do" all her life, I found even her wedding gifts unused, stashed away "for a rainy day." When my father died, having dreamed for years of going to Europe, there was more than sufficient money in an envelope marked "My Future Trip." It was too late. There was no "present" left for the future to gobble.

An exercise suggested by such pathos I call sacramental pampering. Readers who are already self-indulgent had best hurry on to the next spirit type. This one is for those of us who would feel guilty doing anything unabashedly for ourselves. I am struck by the story of the woman who took an expensive ointment, probably costing much of what she had saved, and poured it on the head of Jesus. For much of my life I would have been the indignant disciple: "Why this waste? For this ointment might have been sold for a large sum, and given to the poor" (Matt. 26:8–9). Jesus' response is special. She has done "a beautiful thing to me" (v. 10).

One of Paul's great illuminations is that the incarnation continues. "Do you know that you are God's temple and that God's Spirit dwells in you?" So certain is he of this sacredness that he threatens any who fail to see it: "If any one destroys God's temple, God will destroy [that person]. For God's temple is holy, and *that temple you are*" (1 Cor. 3:16–17, italics added).

As a first exercise, ask yourself with all due seriousness (self-indulgent though it may sound) what act would most treat your embodied self as if it were in truth the temple of God.

Every morning is a drama in front of a mirror. Usually it is an experiment in pseudo resurrection, shaving or covering the face with an appearance regarded as socially acceptable. As an exercise, some evening begin by reading 2 Corinthians 3:12–18. Then take fifteen minutes before a mirror, looking carefully at your "unveiled face," at every line, the color of eyes and hair, freckles, birthmarks, the way parts of you tend not to behave. This is you. You earned every wrinkle. Each mark has a story, as does vintage furniture. Bless every part. Then take a hot bath by candlelight. As you wash, touch your body as sacred. Use oil as anointment. Feel every inch of your skin, starting with your feet. To accept oneself as fully and wholly accepted by God is a profoundly spiritual act.

What's in a name? Everything. Look up the etymology of your name. Does it fit you? If not, what name would you choose? When monks make their vows, they are often given a new name by which to model their new life. Make such a choice for yourself, after giving sufficient time for the Holy Spirit to suggest a secret name of endearment. Use that name often, especially when on the verge of depression, insecurity, or self-doubt.

Feeling is a form of contemplation. Contemplation as a disciplined capacity for immediacy with the present has spatial implications. This is what gives rare beauty to the Trappist vow of stability. One promises to spend one's life in immediacy with a small acreage of land in which each growing thing is to become one's companion. There is enough mystery in a spoonful of dirt to last a lifetime. Can you make even a token commitment to a place, if only your back yard, and begin an intentional acquaintanceship with each part?

The modern penchant for mobility, planned obsolescence, and the isolated, nuclear family makes it difficult to experience the sacramental stability of things, people, and places. Yet without the warm familiarity of the commonplace, one remains an alien, an outsider, everywhere. One compromise is to become so familiar with the one moving that the moving itself can become a movable feast. That is, one can become one's own sacramental.

Recruit a friend for this experiment. For fifteen minutes, each of you study your own hand, front and back. Then take fifteen minutes, opposite each other, to study each other's hands. Though one may know this in theory, it is startling to see how different each of us is. It is simply not true that a finger is a finger, or that to see the lines of one palm is to have seen them all. Claiming such specialness begins the process of rendering the self sacramental.

With that friend or another, stare into each other's eyes. Become totally present, available. Be prepared to feel very uncomfortable, probably embarrassed, even pained. Our individualistic culture socializes us to avoid eye contact, especially with strangers, suspecting that it borders on invasion. Before beginning the exercise, give each other permission to break this taboo for a preset period of time. Here one can enter a sacramental depth that is bottomless.

The Buddhist tradition provides helpful exercises in the discipline of intensifying the immediate.[4] To begin, take a walk with the intent of becoming totally mindful. Be attentive to your feet, watching the toe as it comes forward and recedes. Then the legs, in common rhythm. Note your diaphragm heaving, your lungs emptying and filling, the passage of air through each nostril. Be sensitive to the diversity of feelings—the tiredness, the stiffness, an itch, a dryness. Pass knowingly in and out of smells. Acknowledge increasingly every bit of what is happening: I am seeing, my toe is pinched, I feel the sun burning, now I am thinking, left foot/ right foot, tight trousers. Do all this with only one instruction: Walk mindfully.

Such a controlled exercise develops skill in action/reflection. Our lives are lived too often as action without reflection and reflection without action. The goal here is to intersect the two as much as possible. I am my experience made conscious. Once this technique is developed, one can use it with any activity. Thus, in my case, I am sitting, my breathing is slowing, I feel coolness against the arm of the chair, my sweater itches, I am becoming content. The intent is to concentrate solely on the "now," gradually expanded until the "here" becomes all.

Thus, in my contentedness I begin to acknowledge wishes and needs as they poke at the edges. I would like this chair to rock. I feel hungry. I think this exercise is ridiculous. Now I feel guilty. Enlarge the perimeters of awareness by becoming attentive to the distinct sounds of this moment. Rest in each; rest in all. Then mix in the sights. Add the touches. Have the smells for dessert.

With practice, enlarge the time period in which you are committed to total mindfulness. To be totally present, luminously aware of everything flooding each moment, is to experience each moment as being unlike any other moment that ever existed. The more open to this instantaneous bombardment, the more radiantly alive one feels. There is a fresh incarnation in flesh, each self a reverent guest in a creation gloriously sacramental.

4. Music

If none of this makes sense, listen to *An American in Paris*. Gershwin provides the experience vicariously, purely in sound. Other music that can give a taste for this spirit type includes Copland's *Appalachian Spring*, Smetana's *The Moldau*, Mussorgsky's *Pictures at an Exhibition*, Richard Strauss's *Domestic* Symphony, Beethoven's Symphony No. 6 ("The Pastoral"), and Grofé's *Grand Canyon Suite*.

5. *Meditation*

Words that might begin one's personal meditative list include: sacred, water, gift, commonplace, earth, sacramental, rare, fire, gratuitous, fondness, domesticity, unique, sanctify, consecrate, shroud, air, blessing, rite, communion, temple, altar, baptism, bell.

6. *Poetry*

This spirit mode is particularly available for those with native poetic sensitivities. The rest of us need periodic immersion in good poetry, rehearsing our attention to metaphor. Such winks of innuendo invite us to be cosmic eavesdroppers. Otherwise, Rilke insists, we languish in the sin of spectatorship in the midst of a world incarnate.

> And we, spectators, always, everywhere,
> looking at, never out of, everything![4]

To "look out of" is incarnation. And it is type 8 that births this sacramental posture of seeing from within, as "outgazing." The poet's approach to life's enigmas, then, becomes understandable: "I will solve my riddle to the music of the lyre" (Ps. 49:4).

Which poets feed which persons is an individual matter. Yet let me suggest, as some of my favorites, Emily Dickinson, A. E. Housman, William Butler Yeats, Robert Frost, Wallace Stevens, William Carlos Williams, Edna St. Vincent Millay. For the adventuresome, there are T. S. Eliot and Gerard Manley Hopkins.

7. *Painting*

Whereas in type 7 we experience playful delight with anything, here gestalts are more central. One is touched by a relational depth opened through illuminating configurations. Form hints sacramentally of universality, in which one sees "all" in "each" — a glance for all glances, a season for all seasons. That, in its own way, is what art is about.

Not surprisingly, this spirit mode emerges well through the paintings of Vermeer.[5] Their small size models the humble quietness of their commonday subject matter. Here one experiences the domesticity of being, the dignity of the simple, which blesses common things with an uncommon sacredness. Vermeer is in love with things and with the unassuming motions that render them sacramentals. This capacity for relations, secretly personal, turns a daily pouring of milk into a eucharistic act, as simple gestures become hints of eternal signs (for example, *The Milkmaid* or *Woman Weighing Gold*).

In such paintings, I-thouness entails a gaze that loves things into being. It establishes a relationship through which one knows by being known. Smooth and warm interior textures caress things into the tranquillity of belonging, fondling the inner integrity of solitary figures into a rare still life. This is the spirit type in which the world's alien strangeness is rendered into gracious fireside warmth. Things become manageably human-size, as if mementos in a woodcutter's cottage, domesticated into a delicious threadbareness of familiarity.

An Anticipation

Merton's deepening participation in Mystery as the Ground of Being (type 1) awakened him increasingly to experience God as priest, whose cosmic liturgies sanctify creation's mysteries. Near the end of his life, these divinely sacramental gestures became distilled for him in the image of a "cosmic dance." Here dance moves from being for its own sake (as in type 3) into being a foretaste of final vision. In such movement, he takes us to the edge of the final spirit type, where the ache of the sacramental universe for consummation is experienced as call. Hints of such consummation come

> when we are alone on a starlit night; when by chance we see the migrating birds in autumn descending on a grove of junipers to rest and eat; when we see children in a moment when they are really children; when we know love in our own hearts; or when, like the Japanese poet Basho, we hear an old frog land in a quiet pond with a solitary splash—at such times the awakening, the turning inside out of all values, the "newness," the emptiness and the purity of vision that make themselves evident, provide a glimpse of the cosmic dance.[6]

11

Imagination and the Dream as Mission

Type 9: Call

At the end of our last section, we saw how sacramentality (type 8) can make overtures toward a unitary vision of transfiguration. This vision is traditionally conceptualized into a doctrine of the "kingdom." Using more inclusive language, there emerge such images as the reign, rule, or commonwealth of God. At its fullest, this spirit type suggests a large orchestra accompanying a huge choir in singing the "Hallelujah Chorus" from Handel's *Messiah*. The central words are these: "The kingdom of the world has become the kingdom of our Lord and of his Christ, and he shall reign for ever and ever" (Rev. 11:15). This spirit type focuses on this vision of God's creativity as "call."

Scripture as a whole, and its final book in particular, envisages creation as a Divine-human wedding. Such a dream brings us face to face with the power of mission. But the goal of history yet to be is not isolated from proleptic moments, foretastes, and glimpses, which God provides all along the divine-human trek. These are at the heart of the final spirit type we are exploring. Such experiences serve as apertures by which to see, albeit through a glass darkly, the vision of the cosmos in which God shall be All in all.

Homecoming

My first introduction to this dimension came early. Each fall my small-town church had a festival called "homecoming." A basement, normally smelling of mildew, was transformed by the excitement of crepe-paper streamers and carved pumpkins. Folks returned whom I had never seen before. A bishop picked me up and fed me a doughnut. While I did not understand many of the words, I somehow knew on such a day that our forgotten little church was important, and that whatever we were about had to have lasting significance.

I understand the words now, and the feel has become expansive. The whole history of the church was contained in the rhythm of that basement: by recalling the past, there is renewed in the present a sense of calling, in anticipation of a goal that flows back from the future as meaning for the whole. Many colleges and organizations retain secularized versions of this homecoming dream, for they too sense that having the perimeter of only a "now" is deadly. Expressed liturgically, this spirit mode is about ingathering. Expressed experientially, it is a taste for that perfect freedom in which "all things are light and joy because all are seen and tasted in and for God" as their end.[1]

Imagination as Spirit

The arts are helpful in portraying this spiritual dimension. They place us in the presence of hope defying fact, through an imagination that refuses premature limits. The various art forms are latent models for "the assurance of things hoped for, the conviction of things not seen" (Heb. 11:1). One can perceive this in a colored pencil guided by the stubby fingers of a child, with turned tongue protruding between determined lips, as a protest against life stifled by a closed and philistine givenness. Imagination is the appetite that coaxes reality into deeper water than tiptoes can handle.

The spirituality we are trying to touch is one through which the world is so baptized in novelty that one's playful frenzies become efforts to fashion the world as a theater fit for the Divine glory. While I experience artists hungering for this fullness, they would be embarrassed by such hyperbole. Yet they and we wither with less. Myopia of the imagination is a fatal disease, stifling both workshop and church, for without vision the people perish. Thus, imagination needs spiritual rooting, lest the commonplace things bathed in promise become not foretastes, but diversions. Faith is the insistence that what is real is what the Divine-human imagination is inviting reality to become—as call. Otherwise, both artist and priest are doomed to "painting" cause and effect with gaudy colors.

Art is not yet reality—but it deserves to be. That is why its various expressions tend to push toward this final spirit mode. Art is grounded in imagination as the point where Spirit and spirit touch, relating to the earth much as promise relates to creativity. When that intersection is recognized, "Cosmos" becomes the title of God's self-portrait. Then each of our creative acts, no matter how small, is seen as preparation for and paraphrase of the Whole.

The Trinity as Plot

We return explicitly, now, to the Trinity from which our journeying began. As our chart portrays, this final spirit type brings together organically all the modes. That is why there is a diagonal arrow across the whole, pointing into this type. The Spirit as Sanctifier blesses creation by calling everything into the fullness of being. Thereby Incarnation, as the Divine-human covenant of cocreativity, gives flesh to the eternal pregnancy of God as primal Abyss, moving toward consummation.

Just saying that is a big order. Perhaps it can be said more simply. Life in the Spirit as Sanctifier means loving self, world, and God into being—together. In an important way, this last spirit mode is the final chapter disclosing the plot of the whole story as one of mutual pilgrimage. The plot is the movement from Abyss to Consummation. Perhaps Paul said it best: "For from [God] and through [God] and to [God] are all things. To [God] be glory for ever. Amen" (Rom. 11:36). Thus the Eucharist comes to its climax when the celebrant lifts the elements skyward, symbolic of the whole universe, and sings: "Through him, with him, in him, in the unity of the Holy Spirit, all glory and honor is yours, almighty Father, for ever and ever." And all of creation thunders, "Amen."[2]

This affirmation brings us to a disclosure at the heart of human nature. Who was the God who created us in God's own image? It was the One who had just spread out a billion stars upon the naked canvas of nothingness, who choreographed personally the sea monsters, and as encore taught the birds to sing a cappella. It is our nature, then, because it is God's, to be creators. Thus it is no surprise that scripture describes our first appearance on the cosmic stage as a dress rehearsal. Greeting and introducing us as apprentice playwrights, God invites us to assign parts to everything in creation, by giving them names (Gen. 2:15–20). Then God designs the set. It resembles a garden. Our part is to improvise as gardeners. When all is ready, he names the theater. It is called Eden, meaning "delight."

The Artist God

The God in whose image we are created, then, is not an engineer but an Artist. Thus we are not born with blueprints stuffed in each pocket, hired to puzzle over how Tab A is supposed to fit into Slot A. Baptism is our artist's license. And here the analogy becomes pointed. Artists do not discover some truth and then paint a picture about it. Artists do not draw a conclusion about life and then communicate it in a poem. Painters are not illustrators, and poets are not essayists. The meaning of the painting is in the act of painting, and the truth of a poem is the poem itself. Thus creation is discovery, and discovery is creation—as a mutual love affair in flesh.

The creative process is badly misunderstood, then, if one asks the novelist, "What did you mean by that novel?" The meaning *is* the novel, and both we and the novelist stand together as if before a mystery. As such, Melville's interpretation of *Moby Dick* may not be any more authoritative than the meaning discerned by the serious reader. Publication is an invitation for us to enter reverently the world of that novel, discussing and arguing together in the corridors of its action about what it might mean.

By analogy, spirit type 9 is our invitation into the cosmic plot that creation is making public. The significance of this cosmic drama is not known previous to its being acted out, not even by God. There are no definitive program notes antecedent to the creativity, nor can one read last night's drama critic's review so that history resembles a repeat performance. The meaning of God's cosmos *is* the cosmos, experienced in this spirit mode of creativity as codiscovery, intertwined with hopes as dreams. The pluralism of God and the pluralism of the cosmos intersect as Incarnation, fashioning a face for each other in the dynamic of Sanctification as homecoming. Such homecoming is to a place we have never been before.

Soon, Very Soon

Calling is at the heart of this spirit type, emerging as vision. This vision is not reserved for the "shakers and movers," those most graphically immersed in midwifing society. Jesus was clear. It is for all. And those who seem to improvise the role best do so in giving drink to the thirsty, food to the hungry, shelter to the stranger, clothing to the naked, with an uncanny sense for where the prison keys are kept. These are the ones with eyes to behold the whole in each part. Thus, in the simplest of gracious acts, they perceive that the Creator's thirst, too, is being slaked, the Redeemer's hunger fed, and the earth made a fit home for the Spirit.

Even mystics, such as John of the Cross, who participate deeply in spirit modes intent on losing the self in God, grasp the fleshly consummation of this final spirit type: "My beloved is the mountains, the solitary wooded valleys, strange islands."[3] One sentence in Christianity's central prayer distills this spirituality of vision: "Thy kingdom come . . . *on earth* as it is in heaven" (Matt. 6:10, italics added).

This spirit type can easily be lost, in two contrasting ways. The first is through spiritualizing the kingdom, or God's commonwealth, into otherworldliness. The second is to dissipate it into future remoteness. Jesus was clear not only about the earthiness of the vision; his parables concerning God's reign also had "soon" as his favorite mood. His metaphors echo the same tense. Instead of choosing images of wine or wood, both of which require aging, Jesus preferred leaven, which takes only hours, or mustard seeds, known for their quick growth into bushes the size of trees (Luke 13:18–21). God's commonwealth is neither apart, remote, nor gradual. It is concrete, proximate, and total—for "the kingdom of God is in the midst of you" (Luke 17:21).

Sin as Spiritualization and as Retail

This final spirit type, then, exposes sins of two kinds. The first is "spiritualization." In spite of the carnal nature of Christianity, rooted as it is in Incarnation, the church has been tempted throughout its history to minimize the earthly. As a result, the created order becomes discounted, and the bodily richness of the self dissipated. Detachment is an important discipline, but for the Christian this dare not mean disengagement from either the world or the self. Detachment is from that ego obsession which destroys relationship through possessiveness. Unless this ego preoccupation be purged, the call to "midwife with" is trivialized into a "doing for." And daily interaction, in time, reduces even such "doing for" to the competitive stance of "doing to." Thus it is that mutual becoming is swallowed up in a win/lose contest, with victory as domination mistaken for vision as wholeness.

When the self as subject thus reduces the "other" to object, both are lost, for everything is drawn into the orbit of one's own center. From such a center, creation's groanings become not a call for transfiguration but a threatening pathos of lament. Without vision, the people perish—into themselves. Without vision, the creation perishes—into otherness. Without vision, "incompleteness" as an invitation into creativity becomes a final incompleteness—which stalks us like a plague.

The second sinful tendency we can call "retailness." One evening, at Princeton, the novelist William Faulkner agreed to answer questions after giving a guest lecture. A conservative Christian student belligerently got to his feet. "Mr. Faulkner, I am disturbed that in your novels God doesn't seem to enter much into the personal lives of your characters." The novelist did not even take a breath: "I have always thought God to be in the wholesale, not the retail business."

Some of the other spirit types we explored dealt, in effect, with God as retailer. But type 9 is insistent on God as wholesaler. That is, while God is a fine portrait painter, with a penchant for detail, here God is encountered as the One who loves to work with a huge brush, about the width of the Milky Way. The importance of a pluralistic spirituality becomes more clear now. We are not forced to choose between two such understandings.

As a corrective to the crass individualism of our times, however, this final spirit type may need special underscoring. Doing so with a red pencil means forfeiting God as cosmic bellhop, one who specializes in providing hot and cold running room service for our whims. Instead, we are opened to a God who is fascinated with bulldozers.

Holy Desire

We must make it our business, said Saint Augustine, "to desire the divine vision" as "an exercise in holy desire." In fact, not seeing "what you long for" becomes "the very act of desiring [that] prepares you." This spirit mode, then, distills what it means to live between the times. On one side of us is the power of vision, the "now" as fervent call to make transfiguration actual. On the other end is the tug of the "not-yet." "Simply by making us wait," Augustine insisted, "God increases our desire, which in turn enlarges the capacity of our soul, making it able to receive what is to be given to us."[4]

Paul lived such spiritual tension through the torque of "call"— "forgetting what lies behind and straining forward to what lies ahead" (Phil. 3:13). In doing so, the torque becomes paradox—for the call is gift, the effort is promise, the doing is waiting, and the old promises are confirmed as new beginnings. "Work out your own salvation with fear and trembling; for God is at work in you, both to will and to work for [God's] good pleasure" (Phil. 2:12–13).

Here one comes finally to know that the more profoundly personal one's spirituality, the more deeply corporate is its vision. This spiritual mode is a holy desire for the transfiguration of the entire cosmos, from which not one blade of grass is to be excluded. " 'Whom shall I send . . . ?' . . . 'Here am I! Send me.' . . . 'How long, O Lord?' " (Isa. 6:8, 11). For as long as a dream can last.

EXERCISES

1. *Sacred Daydreaming*

I long felt "unspiritual." The models that my introvert parents bequeathed me, an extrovert, were variations on type 1. But my body refused all kindly suggestions to be still, and there seemed to be no mantra capable of getting my mind to shut up. I can now pinpoint the problem. From my parents' spiritual perspective, my imagination has congenital indigestion. Even now, I am hardly ten minutes into a service of worship before I have redesigned the church architecturally, provided alternative lighting, painted the nave, found new hymns, and provided an alternative melody for the anthem.

Therefore, a spiritual breakthrough came for me when the idea of spiritual pluralism proposed that imagination be baptized as a spiritual capacity. My logic was simple. If the divine image in us is of God as Creator, then imagination is a central talent that we share with God.

Greek is a language that defines things in terms of what they *have* been. In Hebrew, however, things are what they *shall* be. So it is in this spirit mode. Still, to see futuristically whatever is before one takes discipline. Especially is this true today, for the modern "prison-houses" built of inertia, depression, oppression, and indifference have foundations made of atrophied imagination.

Try some of these exercises as a diuretic for the imagination:

- Take any word. Enrich it by listing as many synonyms for it as you can. Make as many puns with them as possible.
- Name a color; in three minutes, list as many things as you can that are characterized by that color.

- Walk around in a room of your house. How many different furniture arrangements can you imagine? Take some graph paper. Draw the outline of each room on a separate sheet. Cut out pieces representing the size of your furniture. Play with them, experiencing all the possibilities opened by this fruit-basket upset. Consider new functions for some of the rooms. If the White House can have an "Oval Room" and a "Lincoln Room," why not yours? Name your rooms. What color changes would provide exciting contrasts and correlations? You have permission for your imagination to tear out walls. Is there a way to let in sun or to create a view? What if you could build an addition, patio, walkway, deck, garden, reflecting pool?
- Check out books from the library on award-winning homes, on remodeling houses, on redecorating, on creative lighting, on Japanese gardens, on landscaping, and on outdoor living. Dream.
- Acquire an ambience tape and hope for the best.
- Find some books on photography. Find out who Ansel Adams is.
- Drive to a section of the city where "it is not safe to be"—one of those "invisible" sections carefully avoided on the Chamber of Commerce tours. Let yourself feel deeply and imaginatively whatever you begin feeling.
- Climb a hill overlooking a city. Sit there.
- Look through picture books on great architecture, on travel.
- Acquire at least one copy of *Sojourners* magazine and some of the mission materials provided by your denomination. Place them side by side with the posters and tour brochures provided by a travel agent.
- Spend time with a globe of the world. Find your house on it.
- Keep company for at least fifteen minutes with the nightly show put on by the stars. Each performance is an opening night. If bored, redesign the Milky Way.
- Whatever context you find yourself in, listen; let it speak for itself.

This is birthing. It is of God. God too is being birthed, with countless faces. How many can you name?

2. Discernment

Individual: Significant decisions that the Christian needs to make are not to be based on personal preferences. They are to emerge as responses to the lurings of Spirit. This discernment by an individual can be helped through a series of steps:

- Pray that your own self-interest will be minimized during the process, surrendering yourself to being led by God.
- With a pencil and paper, describe as clearly as you can the decision that you need to make.
- List the parts—the why, when, who, where, hows. Take your time. After each of these steps, take a "break" so that your "thinking" can shake down into "feeling tones." Respect your hunches—of not-quiteness, of peace, of "Really?"
- Remove the concentric layers wrapped around the issue, tending to make it a problem. Thus, for example, the "issue" of whether or not to take a new job in another city may turn out to be, in fact, the "dilemma" of freedom and responsibility for an ailing parent.
- On one side of a page, list the reasons that might lead you toward a positive decision. On the other side, list reasons why a negative response might be preferable. Keep this page with you for a while, adding to it until you sense that you have done enough.
- Choose the right time and place. Light a candle as symbol that you are not alone in this. Ask for guidance. Read all that you have written. Underline what particularly "speaks" to you. Sit quietly and feel deeply. Record what emerges— images, thoughts, feelings, leadings. Remain there until what you experience begins to be variations on the themes already heard. Summarize what has emerged.
- You may be finished. Do not act immediately, but live with the decision for a while. If you are not ready, take another session in which you return to whatever stage feels incomplete. Repeat as necessary.

Individual with Group: Further help in learning to discern the nuances of the Spirit's leadings comes from the Quaker tradition. One exercise is called the "Clearness Session." When someone feels the need for special guidance, that person calls together four to six persons whose spiritual sensitivity is trusted. Before coming together, they are given in writing the question to be discerned, as well as relevant background information. In the group session itself, they listen carefully as the person shares everything that might be germane. The task of the group is to ask clarifying questions and to provide feedback about what is heard, without giving opinions, advice, or conclusions. Persons may suggest assignments, but the decision belongs to the individual. There can be one session or a series over a planned period of time. Such sessions are exercises in birthing under promise. Parker Palmer calls such times "startling," for the answer is almost always within the person, needing only to be drawn out.[5]

Group: Richard Foster wisely recognizes that the church is not supposed to be a democratic institution. It is a theocracy of the Spirit. Our task is to discern the workings of Spirit with spirit, not to vote on personal opinions, nor to permit a tyranny of the majority.[6] The Jerusalem Conference, meeting to decide the future of Christianity's world mission, reached its conclusion by discerning what "seemed good to the Holy Spirit and to us" (Acts 15:28). Experiment with such a discernment process—in personal, family, and church decision-making.

When corporate discussion over an issue becomes intense, heated, or unduly political, the Sisters of Loretto permit anyone to call for a period of silence, usually three to five minutes in length. It is remarkable what clarity can occur. Quakers will often use such silence to gain "a sense of the meeting."

The Jesuits have recently suggested structures for group discernment, based on the exercises of Ignatius of Loyola. One possibility is this: When an issue of consequence is to be considered by a group, informational materials are provided for each person prior to the meeting. Before reading them, individuals are to prepare themselves spiritually, asking for illumination and for the strength to get their egos out of the way. Then the materials are studied, making sure not to come to a decision. The purpose of such preparation is for each person to come to the session with an informed and open mind.

The first group session focuses on the use of imagination. Writing on newsprint, the group as a whole, or in sections, brainstorms options without regard for practicality. This session is followed by a period of prayer for illumination concerning the options uncovered. The group then distills the list into a more practical, manageable handful of options. Then, again using newsprint, everyone enters into an exercise of suggesting the pros, then the cons, for each option. No person is to repeat any point already made, to make out a case for any particular option, or to state a personal opinion.

When this is done, each person goes off alone, reviewing the options prayerfully and asking for discernment. Upon return, persons are numbered off randomly in groups of three to five for sharing, the results from which are reported in a meeting of the whole. A straw vote may be taken to gain a sense of the group. A consensus may have occurred. If not, the process is continued as long as any persons feel strongly that their discernment has not been heard or that the group has not yet considered the options in sufficient depth.[7]

3. *Spiritual Direction*

"Rule" means straightedge—that by which all else is measured. From the beginning, the Christian tradition has recognized the need for a rule against which one's life can be held accountable to the vision. Israel had the Ten Commandments, as a summary of the law, as rule. Matthew distilled from the teachings of Jesus the Beatitudes as rule. And Paul did the same for his churches by enumerating the characteristics of the Spirit. It is not surprising, then, that in time the church would develop more detailed rules for measuring Christian life, such as the Rules of Benedict, Augustine, Francis, and Wesley.[8]

As an exercise, draw a line down the center of a piece of paper. On one side, list categories expressive of your primary spheres of living (such as job, family, friends, groups). Leave space under each. Then summarize briefly how you are living out each part. On the other side of the page, place in creative tension what you take to be the Christian vision for that arena. After spending time with the tension between the left side and the right, list several realizable changes reflective of greater faithfulness. Will you promise to be held accountable to them? How? Some persons may prefer to list the vision first, followed by the performance. Let these be a transitional rule for you.

Over the next month or so, give attention to developing a more complete Rule, reflecting a vision against which you can periodically appraise your days and your nights. Give consideration to such matters as the rhythm of work and play, use of money and time, type and amount of food and drink (consider fasting), types and frequency of worship, keeping informed, exercise, possessions, exposure to nature and the desert, disciplined spiritual practices, nurture of the intellect, culture and beauty, passion for social justice, sabbatical time, sensuality, sexuality, quality time for your extended family, depth and breadth of relations, balance of sound and silence, sharing who you are and what you have, frequency of scheduled recollection. Do this with an eye to identify-

ing overall criteria, such as simplicity, priority, witness, enthusi-
asm, and commitment.

Individual Direction: There is no such thing as a solitary Christian. Even hermits take the scripture, prayers, and daily office of
the community with them. An expression of this social nature of
spirituality is the widespread use of "spiritual directors" throughout Christian history. One may prefer such names as spiritual
friend, prayer partner, or soul companion. I experienced this
phenomenon first when ten years ago a colleague asked for an
hour of my time—time, I thought, in which I would function as
counselor. To my surprise, he shared what was happening to him
without once raising a problem for which he was seeking solution.
Finally he just stopped and asked simply, "What do you hear me
saying?" That was a request for spiritual direction.

Therapy is a method for emotional healing when the pain or
dysfunction threatens to become debilitating. *Counseling* is a
means of support and dialogue for a person needing to make
and/or live with one or more crucial decisions. My colleague was
asking for neither of these. *Spiritual direction* occurs when the
individual requests a sensitive companion for the journey, one
willing to become involved in a process of mutual discernment of
the Spirit's lurings. The real Spiritual Director is the Holy Spirit,
with one's companion helping to midwife the vision being birthed
concretely through the imagination. For this, my friend was
asking.

This was a role played by the prophets for Israel's kings, as, for
example, when Nathan mirrored David back to himself in a story
of deadly judgment. When Nathan used the analogy of a wealthy
person with many sheep stealing the solitary sheep of a poor man,
the king in anger shouted: "The man who has done this deserves
to die." Nathan replied: "You are the man" (2 Sam. 12:1–7).

Although Jesus called many, he was spiritual director for a
smaller group, centering around the Twelve. Paul played this role
for the churches he founded, through periodic visits and letters.
In the early centuries, Christians came to the desert, asking of the
saintly hermits living there, "Abba, a word for my soul." Abbas, in
so functioning, became "abbots," and around them were drawn
communities for spiritual discernment and growth. These came
to be called monasteries.

In time, monasteries expanded this practice into schools. The
word "school" comes from *schola*, meaning "leisure." Universi-
ties, first developed around monasteries, provided the leisure for

discerning the meaning of one's life, within interrelated contexts such as philosophy, history, and science. Something of this intent is preserved in England, where each student has a tutor who functions as a guide for the pilgrimage.

Luther, a product of such monastic discernment, expanded the practice still further by insisting on the functional "priesthood of all believers." Wesley, in turn, made this contribution concrete by recognizing group spiritual direction as a mandatory part of Christian discipleship, organizing "societies" around spiritual direction "classes," with "bands" for more rigorous discipline.

In our time, there is a renewed recognition of this need for soul companions in the faith. This can begin by taking seriously "God-parents" at baptism and "sponsors" in confirmation training, moving toward *koinonia* groups in which the pastor functions as director of directors. Without lifelong accountability in the face of the Christian vision, spiritual disciplines not only lose their perspective as means, but are dissipated into having no more staying power than New Year's resolutions.

There are as many "techniques" for providing spiritual direction as there are directors, yet they are all variations on the theme of creative listening, that is, discernment. Incarnation provides the model:

> Empathy is the process of placing oneself in the frame of reference of another, perceiving the world as the other perceives it, sharing his or her world imaginatively. Incarnation means that God assumes our frame of reference, entering into our human situation of finitude and estrangement, sharing our human condition even unto death.[9]

A spiritual friend is one who so enters your life that she or he can sing your song when you have forgotten the words—and will know whether, at the moment, it needs to be sung in a minor or a major key.

How does one start doing "direction"? My colleague was right in knowing the question to be raised: "What do you hear?" The spiritual friend helps in discerning motifs, recurring patterns, avoidances, revealing signs of dis-ease, sudden excitements, potential insights, and callings—not "for" but "with." Thus the spiritual companion is a midwife of vision, involved in the lifelong process of its birthing.

In functioning as spiritual director, ask nonleading questions, intent on evoking further sharing. Repeat phrases back, inviting expansion. Ask questions for clarification. After careful listening, you might try such comments as "Do I hear you saying . . . ?" And later still, one might venture a few statements that begin, "Could it be . . . " or "I wonder if . . . " At the end of each session, an assignment is often helpful, to be done before the next session. The right assignment often emerges by asking the person directly what she or he senses would be most helpful. The name for the process throughout is "visioning."

It is usually helpful to form a contract between the two persons, making a commitment concerning frequency and length of meetings, the overall time period, and the type of direction that is being requested. Options concerning type could be "existential" (discernment through the sharing of one's "here and now"), or the focus can be on the quality of one's prayer life or the development of one or more spiritual disciplines. Or a portion of the church year can serve as its structure, for example, working one's way through a Lenten pilgrimage into Easter.[10]

Mutual direction is also possible, even done over a meal in a special place. It is essential, however, that a decision be made at the beginning of each session as to who is to go first—thereby keeping the roles of director and directed distinct. Before shifting these roles, take a break, thereby marking the reversal of function. A key characteristic of direction appears by contrasting it with friendly conversation. In the latter, there is a fluctuating focus, much as in tennis: "What you just said about you reminds me of the time when I . . . " In direction, the ball remains on the same side of the net: "Does that relate to what you were telling me last time?"

Direction by mail is also possible. This can be coupled with journaling. The two persons involved draw a line down the middle of each page of their respective loose-leaf journals. They are thus able to send portions of their journals, as appropriate, with the right side of the page available for the friend's comments.

Group Direction: Wesley's important contribution to this spirit type is his development of "Christian conference," that is, group spiritual direction. He forbade his ministers to preach where there would be no society available to provide spiritual direction before they left. These societies were organized into lay-led "classes." In each case, the group of approximately twelve persons provided support and accountability for each person's "growth in grace." A key question was addressed in turn to each person. "What is the state of your soul?" Translated into current idiom, each was asked, "How are you, really?" And the goal? By speaking the truth in love and sharing one another's joys and sorrows, persons were enabled to discern the Christian vision by living as if it were already fact. Central was the vision of "social holiness," as applied to self, neighbor, and society.[11]

As an exercise, choose a form of direction most practically suited to your needs. Often I am asked how to find a director. A ready-made possibility is to contact a monastery or convent in the area. If they do not provide such a service, they are likely to know the possibilities. Denominational headquarters are beginning to acquire the names of persons who have received such training. If left to find one's own spiritual companion, think of one or more persons whom you regard as being insightful and having their lives fairly well in order. Invite one of these to lunch. Share. If the experience feels "right," broach your need and see what happens. It is possible that in finding the right relationship, the word "spiritual" may need to be avoided. Some of the best candidates have been burned by stereotypes of spirituality.

Focused Group Direction: Interestingly, the anatomy of this type of spirituality is receiving widespread application in secular society today. Groups are forming around many activities requiring firmness of resolve in the face of a vision of wholeness, whether the problem is dieting, smoking, alcohol, or drug abuse. In countless such situations, recognition is growing of the need for others through whom to be held accountable to one's vision. The popular concept of co-dependency as living a life of mutual blackmail insists on breaking the vicious circle through responsibility as mutual trust. No one can be midwifed alone—physically, mentally, emotionally, or spiritually.

As an exercise, prioritize several issues in your life for which concrete accountability would be helpful. Consider joining a group whose intention is to provide such "direction." Use the Yellow Pages. If your need is not listed, call Alcoholics Anonymous. They are a helpful resource for all kinds of accountability groups.

4. Pilgrimage

Almost all religions have sacred places to which the faithful are drawn as pilgrims. Catholicism has Rome, Islam has Mecca, Judaism has Jerusalem, Anglicanism has Canterbury, and Protestantism, in spite of itself, has the Holy Land. The abundance of lesser Christian "shrines" reflects the fact that Christians are followers of "the Way" (Acts 9:2). Without symbols of the goal to which the way leads, the Christian's life-style is reduced from pilgrimage to economy tour. It is likely that many vacations are frantic marathons because they are attempts to feed an unacknowledged craving for pilgrimage with quantity rather than quality. As a result, places, rather than a special place, end up substituting doing for being.

Persons die spiritually, and sometimes physically, when they no longer have anything to which to look forward. Attempts at avoiding boredom become boring, with one year distinguished from another by who plays in the Super Bowl.

As an exercise, ask yourself these questions: (1) Where would I go in order to be "home"? (2) What should I see in order to know myself better? (3) What place would be like a dream come true? (4) What one thing should I do before I die in order for my life to have closure? Be concrete. Does a particular place suggest itself as answer to more than one question? Anticipate going there. Plan for it. Go.

What "minor" pilgrimage could be taken soon, as a symbolic variation of your major pilgrimage? For example, if going "home" to Appalachia were my choice, perhaps visiting the mines in southern Missouri some Sunday afternoon would be a beginning. For others, such possibilities might be a cemetery, basilica, river, ethnic restaurant, trail, or abandoned farm. If imagination fails, get a travel book from the library.

5. *The Presence of Growth*

Surround yourself with daily signs of growth, especially those for which responsibility is involved. Because green is the color for Trinity, green plants are particularly appropriate. Develop the practice of sharing plant clippings with other persons. Thus the products of your own loving nurture can grow on the windowsills of others, while the tender care of others, in turn, can find harvest in your home. Bless each plant with the name of the giver.

Whether they are conscious of it or not, gardening for many persons is a deeply liturgical activity. While most spirit modes can be experienced through it, gardening is, above all, a parable of type 9. The pilgrimage is from seed to harvest. I sensed this expansively when my elderly neighbor planted tree seedlings whose shade she would never enjoy.

As a spiritual activity, plan and nurture a garden into being.

Consider symbolically such dimensions as where, with whom, what, for whom. If a garden is impractical, duplicate your kindergarten days, when with awe you watched your own plant grow daily from a seed in a paper cup. Saint Francis, working in his garden, was asked, "What would you do if you knew you had only one more hour to live?" The reply was well chosen: "I would work in my garden."

6. *Nonviolence*

The scriptural treatment of the commonwealth of God describes acts of both doing and waiting. It also involves one thing more—times when the two unite as signal acts of foretaste. These are the tokens of vision, acquired by living *as if* God's reign had begun. Perhaps no act does this better than assertive nonviolence.

Try this exercise. In the light of the following summary of Jesus' teachings, consider your attitudes and actions in each of these areas:

1. your personal relations
2. your functioning as a citizen, and
3. your role as world resident

"You have heard that it was said, 'An eye for an eye and a tooth for a tooth.' But I say to you, Do not resist one who is evil. But if any one strikes you on the right cheek, turn . . . the other also; and if any one would sue you and take your coat, let [that person] have your cloak as well. . . .

"You have heard that it was said, 'You shall love your neighbor and hate your enemy.' But I say to you, Love your enemies and pray for those who persecute you." (Matt. 5:38–40, 43–44)

What changes are you willing to make in your life, both in attitude and in behavior?

In the light of your discernment above, consider the implications for you in taking seriously a "modest proposal for peace" named on a Mennonite poster: "That Christians stop killing each other." In what ways are you willing to work for such a "modest" vision? Be concrete.

7. *Mission*

Read the story of Jesus washing the feet of his disciples (John 13:1–20). Certain Protestant Reformers were so taken by this unique command that they considered making it a third sacrament. Thus one could regard Baptism as the sacrament of creation, Eucharist the sacrament of redemption, and foot washing the sacrament of sanctification—as the call to servanthood.

As Jesus prepared for his final pilgrimage to Jerusalem, he gave last-minute instructions for being "able to drink the cup" of mission (Matt. 20:22): "Whoever would be great among you must be your servant, and whoever would be first among you must be your slave; . . . not to be served but to serve" (vs. 26–28). In Jerusalem, as his final sayings before acting out as model on Golgotha his own servanthood, he annunciated the vision that was to flow back over the whole as dream. Of what shall God's commonwealth be composed?

> Then the righteous will answer him, "Lord, when did we see thee hungry and feed thee, or thirsty and give thee drink? And when did we see thee a stranger and welcome thee, or naked and clothe thee? And when did we see thee sick or in prison and visit thee?" (Matt. 25:37–39)

For those who would see God, the answer sought down through history is finally given: "Truly, I say to you, as you did it to one of the least of these my brethren [and sisters], you did it to me" (Matt. 25:40). God is experienced as foretaste in the dream hinted through the eyes of the hungry as they are fed.

Using imaginatively this image of God's commonwealth, evaluate your day; your week; your year; your life. Make some decisions about priorities.

The sins of omission are often more serious than those of commission. Most persons see themselves as loving persons. Perhaps they are. But the issue is not simply loving, but how broadly. Mafia members tend to be loving of their families, willing even to kill for them. The patriot expands such commitment to the nation. Others may broaden their loving to include their race. But, for the Christian, love as commission is measured against the breadth of one's omission. How broadly should I love? The Christian criterion is direct and uncompromising. Against love as calculated selfishness, no matter how expansive, love is to be universal with the inclusion of enemies the foolproof test.

Who, then, is my neighbor? Whomever one meets. What if I make it a practice to live and work so that I meet only those whom I like and who like me? That won't do. Universality is measured by including "those who spitefully misuse you." How often? Seventy times seven. Really? I'll try, but grudgingly. You missed the point. It is love of *self* that is not to be expanded, but universalized: care for all persons as if they were yourself. What if I don't love myself? Love as you have been loved. And how am I loved? Unto death—remember? Every human on the face of the earth is the one for whom Christ died.

The following exercises may be among the hardest to do honestly. Draw a circle in the middle of a page. With a colored pencil write in the space outside the circle those *kinds* of persons you would prefer not to have inside your "circle of love," whatever that means for you. Be specific. What races would you exclude? Which class of people? What of communists? homosexuals? Be honest. In another color, write those kinds of persons you would exclude from your workplace if you had a choice. In a third color, write those with whom you would feel uneasy sitting in your place of worship. Fourth, indicate those whom you would prefer not to entertain in your home. Finally, ask yourself who would make you uneasy if intimacy developed between them and a member of your family, or a dear friend.

As a second exercise, draw a circle on another piece of paper. Write outside the circle those kinds of *offenses* that would place a person outside your personal circle of forgiveness. Murder? Rape? Atheism? Sabotage? Incest? Child abuse? Using another color, indicate how your list would change if you answered that question not for yourself but as a judge in a court, responsible to execute the options provided by the law. In that capacity, for what kinds of offenses would you be willing to sentence a person to death? Would there be other responses to be considered? What if you were a minister or priest? a governor with the power to grant clemency? Consider the meaning of the differences in your lists.

One thing remains to be done. Reconsider these exercises from the perspective of Jesus. What would his answers likely have been? In answering, consider his teachings, such as the one about the person without sin being the one to cast the first stone. What would the implications be if one took seriously Paul's vision that in Christ there is neither Jew nor Greek, slave nor free, male nor female, "for you are all one in Christ Jesus"? (Gal. 3:28). Your answers may also be affected by Paul's insistence that the Christian is one loved by God not because that person is better than anyone else, "for there is no distinction; since all have sinned and fall short of the glory of God, they are justified by his grace as a gift" (Rom. 3:22–24). Should being a Christian, rather than simply a "person of goodwill," make a difference in how one answers?

After your considerations in the light of such Christian "ideals," ask yourself in all seriousness how practical the Christian vision really is.

Some of us regard ourselves as liberal because we are willing for others to have what we have, to live where we live, to participate in our life-style, as long as their educational, cultural, and economic level is the same as ours. Where the Christian vision becomes tense, however, is when it requires sacrifice of one's own standard of living—having less in order that others who have little may have more.

For this exercise, find five significant symbols that express your "success." Look around your house for important expressions of achievement gained during your long and difficult efforts to "make something of yourself." Take these symbols into your favorite room and surround yourself with them. Then consider your present life-style in the light of these matters:

> *The World Situation:* One fourth of all persons in this country live below the poverty level, and two thirds of the world's population are in a situation of severe malnutrition, bordering on starvation. Yet if every person in the world lived at the socioeconomic level of the average middle-class American, the ecosystem of the earth would collapse under the weight of consumption and waste.

> *Daily Life:* " 'Therefore I tell you, do not be anxious about your life, what you shall eat or what you shall drink, nor about your body, what you shall put on. . . . Which of you by being anxious can add one cubit to [your] span of life?' " (Matt. 6:25–27)

> *Savings and Inheritance:* " 'One thing you still lack. Sell all that you have and distribute to the poor. . . . How hard it is for those who have riches to enter the kingdom of God!' " (Luke 18:22, 24)

> *Motivations for Living:* "Whoever seeks to gain his [or her] life will lose it, but whoever loses [that] life will preserve it." (Luke 17:33)

> *Relation of Faith and Works:* "If a brother or sister is ill-clad and in lack of daily food, and one of you says to them, 'Go in peace, be warmed and filled,' without giving them the things needed for the body, what does it profit? So faith by itself, if it has no works, is dead." (James 2:15–17)

None of us does well in such an exercise. If so, of what significance are such scriptural admonitions? Is it helpful to consider the guilt induced, not as a mark for a final examination failed, but as a source of creative tension with a commonwealth of God still in the making—with our daily answers part of the ingredients?

Read a work on spirituality by a third-world liberation theologian—for example, Gustavo Gutiérrez's *We Drink from Our Own Wells*.[12] Of what significance is it that we in the developed world are working out our spirituality in a contrasting socio-economic context?

8. *Ecology as Prayer*

Long have we referred to the earth as "mother," but treated her as "it." To take without giving is a violation of all relationships. Hosea, regarding the earth in terms of mutual vision, imaged the relation in terms of marriage:

> And in that day, says the Lord, you will call me, "My husband.". . .
> And I will make for you a covenant on that day with the beasts of the field, the birds of the air, and the creeping things of the ground; and I will abolish the bow, the sword, and war from the land; and I will make you lie down in safety. And I will betroth you to me for ever. (Hos. 2:16–19)

To treat all of creation, both inanimate and animate, as family is to transform one's life into prayer.

As an exercise in ecological spirituality, find a piece of earth that is derelict, a place abandoned. While such a corner may not exist on your own property, there are certainly places in your neighborhood, town, or city that are overtaken by trash, weeds, and neglect. Love that piece of God's creation until it takes on the appearance of gift. Interestingly, many local governments have instituted "adopt a highway" programs for individuals or groups. The church's equivalent might be a spirituality of adoption in which a piece of the earth is reclaimed as part of the divine garden. Whatever part you choose, restore it as fit for walking with God in the cool of the evening.

If your time is limited, at least pick up the trash as a symbolic act of atonement. My candidate for sainthood is a friend whose love of the earth is such that he goes home at night with pockets and briefcase filled with assorted trash he has gathered along the way. Do they give Nobel Prizes for being a scavenger for Christ?

If all goes well, *Voyager 2*, around the year 4200, will pass within 1.7 light-years of the star Ross 248. Orbiting around this star might be a planet with intelligent life. If by chance its inhabitants could retrieve the *Voyager*, they would hear the voice of President Carter: "This is a present from a small, distant world. We are attempting to survive our time so we may live into yours." Whether we do or not is a spirit issue. That future may well rest on how deeply we are in love with those sounds of our planet that were sent by tape along with the *Voyager:* "Thunder clapping and frogs croaking and a newborn baby cooing and crying."[13] Make your own tape, placing on it the sounds of those things best able to capture the vision of the earth in foretaste of its fullness, to which you are called.

9. *Hagiology*

Almost from its beginning, the church has honored those who have given their life for the Christian vision, either by quality of living or by selflessness of dying. Hagiology is the name for the calendar of such saints and events, with recognition awarded, for the most part, on the day of their death—as their second birthday. Monks take the name of such a saint, and dedicate their living to each day's saint as model.

In living the dream of the new heaven and the new earth, it is crucial that one does not feel alone, but "surrounded by so great a cloud of witnesses" (Heb. 12:1). Therefore start your own hagiology, beginning with selections from an official list. Add important persons and events in your own pilgrimage—international, national, ecclesiastical, cultural, personal—both sacred and secular.

As an example, the following are from my own hagiology for the first few days of December:

1. Charles Foucauld, Algeria (1916); Rosa Parks keeps her seat (1955)
2. Four nuns murdered in El Salvador, 1980 (Donovan, Kazel, Clarke, Ford); Aaron Copland (1990)
3. Francis Xavier (1552); R. L. Stevenson (1894); Renoir (1919)
4. Council of Trent ends (1563); massacre of Chicago Black Panthers (1969); Benjamin Britten (1976)
5. Mozart (1791); Monet (1926)

10. *Meditation*

Words worth considering in beginning a list for meditation include wedding, foretaste, eschatology, cocreation, vision, creativity, enemy, process, beatific vision, success, kingdom, commonwealth, queendom, banquet, garden, judgment, glory, rule, feast, benediction, alleluia.

11. *Music*

Mahler composed his *Resurrection* Symphony for the occasion of this spiritual type. Of it he wrote in the program, "All creation adorns itself continuously for God. Everyone therefore has only one duty, to be as beautiful as possible in every way in the eyes of God and [people]." Those who would like to hear other versions of this vision are invited to listen to Purcell's trumpet voluntaries, Bach's *Christmas Oratorio*, Wagner's "Good Friday Spell" from *Parsifal*, Beethoven's Symphony No. 9, and most of Handel's oratorios. Any movement marked Largo is a harbinger of this spirit type.

12. *Scripture as Music*

Reading scripture with either literal or scientific eyes can be lethal. The spirit mode we are exploring requires reading with the eyes of a poet. An excellent exercise in learning to do this comes in letting music and scripture intermingle.

Find a recording of Handel's *Messiah.* Correlate the following selections of music with these scripture passages:

SUFFERING

"Worthy Is the Lamb That Was Slain, Amen"—Romans 8:15–19

DEATH

"The Trumpet Shall Sound"—Psalm 103

RESURRECTION

"I Know that My Redeemer Liveth"—John 20:1–18

NEW HEAVEN AND NEW EARTH

"Hallelujah Chorus"—Revelation 21—22

A further exercise in correlating music and text is listening to (even comparing with one another) one or more of these masterpieces of vision: Brahms's *A German Requiem,* Mozart's *Requiem,* Verdi's *Requiem.*

13. *Painting*

This spirit mode is a foretaste of the beatific vision. T. S. Eliot is right in suggesting that for most of us it occurs only as hints and guesses. To experience the whole is an occupation best fit for the saint. Yet a taste of it is closed to no one.

We discussed van Gogh's paintings as expressions of his call to paint everything with promise. His suicide was the unbearable lovesickness of one intoxicated with, and overcome by, the accumulated ingredients of this vision. His final year was one drawn and quartered by the tension between God as Nothingness and God as Consummation.

After struggling for well over a year to choose a single painting able to hold together creatively this tension as vision, El Greco's *View of Toledo* emerged as my choice. Here the new Jerusalem touches our condition as a somber green, shadowed into black. Yet it is adorned by an edging of emerald, that precious shade reserved for spring after a warm rain. Small figures, as if on pilgrimage, place human life in cosmic perspective. The movement is upward, ascending—yet not to an "elsewhere," for the light, while behind, comes through. The vision is lush yet ominous, immanent but never within our control. It is "in" but not "of," "of" but not yet "in." The "feel" of the cosmos is as gift, yet only so for invited guests on tiptoe. All is silent and still, in an eternal sameness; and yet through it all is a strange pregnancy calling for a midwife. Here Incarnation becomes God's wooing of the virgin city as bride—the commonwealth of God flowering as wedding feast.

To Mary was it promised, "The Holy Spirit will come upon you" (Luke 1:35). Under El Greco's genius, this Magnificat becomes a cosmic chorus. Each speck of earth, as handmaiden of "low degree," is exalted, as the Spirit fills "the hungry with good things." Captured by this final spirit mode, one dares to look with eyes unblurred by tears or pain or death, for the former things are already passing away. "Behold, I make all things new" (Rev. 21:5). Trusting the dream, one can begin over again—and again.

A Summary

In this spirit type, one can feel a whisper of wholeness flow back over all the modes we have explored. It brings closure to the

Christian faith with a diagonal sweep, in which the *Infinite Mystery*, pledged beyond the point of recall to history as the arena of *Incarnation*, lures and calls all toward cocreative completeness, through the nurturing and searing of *Spirit*.

It is this wholeness, in turn, which insists that each spirit type remain unique, forbidding this pluralism to disintegrate into a competitive exclusivity. And having sampled the hors d'oeuvres of a richly pluralistic spirituality, the task that emerges is that of discipline — intentionally practicing trinitarian living into a viable way of life.

Part III

Practicing the Hints
Into Visibility:
Wagering on the Commonplace
as Rare

12

Concluding Morning Glances: To End at the Beginning

I appreciate receiving minutes of meetings. Often I need to be told what, if anything, we accomplished. So permit me to offer this set of scribblings from our time together. We have wandered a bit from the feelings with which we began, but never far. I suspect that what these minutes will do, for both of us, is to make visible as conclusions the working assumptions with which, as hints, we began.

1. Christian spirituality is pluralistic. Perhaps this has been our primary theme. While at first glance such a claim appeared strange, we tramped around enough in Christian history to become surprised that this truth has not been more obvious to the church—especially given its insistence on God as triune. Too often, the only God the average person hears about is one who is too simplistic or too remote to ignite the imagination.

After our times together, you may still find yourself unable to entertain seriously a Christian God. At least, may you have been so marked by the hints of life's possible experiences that your "no" will be wrapped in fond regret. In any case, the kitchen door will be unlocked, and I'll leave the coffeepot on.

2. The Trinity has been traditionally understood as a clue both to the ways in which God functions in the cosmos and to who God is. By resisting the tendency to pose these two understandings as rivals, or to reduce one to the other, we explored their interplay as creative foundation for developing an organic spirituality of multiple types. These types could then be understood as parts of a

whole rather than as exclusively competitive parts of a hierarchy. Our task was so to describe them separately that they became affirmed inclusively.

3. For the Christian, the primary aperture for understanding and validating this pluralistic spirituality was an event in history called Jesus as the Christ. Incarnation is the name for the concrete intersection of these two expressions of Trinity.

Before Christian theology developed sufficiently to conceptualize this revelation with sophistication, the church distilled it dramatically, as the repeatable rehearsal called Eucharist. In that event, the elements of common-day life, elevated into God as ingathering, are empowered and received back for outgiving. Wrapped within this whole event, the sacred crumbs become foretastes of the final ingathering. This Sacrament distills, then, the eternal gestures of Trinity. God as Creator, Redeemer, and Sanctifier is birthing a Divine-human cosmos of corresponding richness.

4. The emergence of varied spirit types through the centuries has been, in reality, a distilling into discipline the experiential dimensions implicit in this primal Christian event. As a result, the dual understandings of Trinity have been identified as grounding the two primary states of our own living: being and doing. These should not be posed as contraries, nor emptied into each other. Instead, just as the interplay of God's being and God's doing emerges as creativity, so these states form the poles of our own spirit life—as being-in-doing and doing-in-being.

5. Spirit life is not rooted in rare experiences. While some persons claim to have had such, I, for one, cannot. Nonetheless, the test is one's response to the first cold light of the morning after.

> What indeed is the enthusiast to do after the first rush of ardor has cooled? How is he or she to explain the sudden departure of that reassuring sense of God's presence? . . . The effort to enter again into the womb of the first experience is doomed by a thinly disguised anxiety.[1]

Interestingly, those who attest to such rare experiences are often those who most insist that spirituality cannot be grounded in them. Teresa of Avila was adamant that spirituality rests on faith alone, in the strength of committed wager. The Gospel of John concurs: "Blessed are those who have not seen and yet believe" (John 20:29).

6. To bet and to wager are different acts. To bet means "to bait," to do something as a way of getting something. Spirituality so

based is unstable, for it depends on measurable consequences. Wager, however, means "pledge," a promise or commitment to do, no matter what. Special experiences, if they do occur, are welcomed gifts, but as unexpected they cannot serve as foundation for one's spirituality.

7. Discipline is that which alone gives the strength to persevere during the dark nights of the silent valleys. It provides "the resources which would yield a positive understanding of the times of spiritual dryness."[2] The intent of this book is to present the wide options of a pluralistic spirituality from which can emerge a tailor-made fabric worthy of such discipline.

8. While discipline is necessary, spirit life is circular. Discipline is neither its end nor its beginning. Hints come first, and ongoing spiritual experience comes after. It is discipline that holds the two together.

Wagering on hints, discipline hones the eyes to see, the ears to hear, and the will to act. Through such rehearsal, one becomes increasingly able to perceive in the commonplace what is indeed "rare," but which would remain common if one had not wagered on such hints as sacred. Faith as commitment means the discipline of practicing common-day hints into visibility by wagering on them as uncommon foretaste. Shrouded in risk, then, all spirituality, for each human being, involves living "as if."

9. None of us is without experiences sufficient to transform one's life spiritually, if wagered on. As to having a "religious base," then, all persons are, more or less, on an equal footing. There are Golgotha times of walking "through the valley of the shadow of death." There are Sinai-like times of mountain ecstasy. The issue is not the experiences themselves, but one's functional assumption as to which are primary and which are diversionary.

Such weighting cannot be avoided. Each of us has already made a faith-wager. Based on some configuration of experience—past, present, hoped for—one lives as if living is worthwhile. Practicing the Presence into visibility, then, may have no more empirical base than the smell of soup, or a bed once friendly made lonely.

10. No matter what its beginning, faith cannot persevere long on memory alone. And so we return full circle to our consistent theme. That which can withstand the erosion of daily commonness is discipline. Since one's spirit base remains always a "nevertheless," the only thing that can defy aridity is a life in obedience to vision. "Faith is the assurance of things hoped for, the conviction of things not seen" (Heb. 11:1). Such conviction-in-hope is

modeled by "those who have their faculties trained by practice" (Heb. 5:14).

11. An analogy may help. No marriage based on the experience of "falling in love" will survive. Nor are odds increased much by a vow to remain wedded partners "for as long as we both are in love." So too in the spiritual life. What alone has a chance to endure is vowed commitment. Although traditional marriage vows verge on idolatry, they are classic for the Divine-human relation called spirituality:

> I, *Name*, take you, *Name*, to be my [spouse],
> to have and to hold
> from this day forward,
> for better, for worse,
> for richer, for poorer,
> in sickness and in health,
> to love and to cherish,
> until we are parted by death.
> —*The United Methodist Hymnal*

12. This makes understandable why the heart of Israel's spirituality is covenant. For the Christian, that covenant is sealed in flesh and blood as Incarnation. Thus while, from our side, spirituality subsists in the practice of faith alone, our wager trusts that it is God's commitment to us that empowers our acts of perseverance. The ability to trust is itself the gift called "grace."

13. Spirituality, as practice, has profound and literal implications for how one sees, hears, touches, smells, and tastes life. It permeates one's total life, wending its way into how one drives a car, the inflections in one's voice, the color and texture of one's clothes, the choice of breakfast cereal.

Thus, encouraging "growth in grace" through the rehearsal of spirit types is not in order to *add* something to daily living. It is to *rebaptize*, and thus purify, one's life-style by making such rehearsed practices "second nature." As orienting dispositions, they come to determine unconsciously the whole texture of one's common-day existence. To use a baseball analogy, a batting slump occurs when a batter's swing no longer feels "second nature" and one has to "try," instead, on each pitch.

14. To use another analogy, an artist's eye is forged by countless hours spent in duplicating the perspectives of the masters, until one is sufficiently disciplined that one's own consistent style emerges from within. Likewise, spiritual formation is practice in

the spirit types of those who have gone before, until through discipline one's own style of spiritual living emerges.

15. This book makes a modest claim. It is a guide suggesting what life might be like if certain hints are lived in the steady gaze of discipline. Thus we end where we began—by remembering with T. S. Eliot that special moments are only "hints followed by guesses, and the rest is prayer, observance, discipline, thought and action."[3] Wesley knew this dialectic well—the discipline of doing until one believes, and believing until one does.

16. Worship is central for spirituality, but for reasons contrary to what is often assumed. Although liturgy does serve as an outlet for feelings, it is more profoundly a rehearsal in *how* to feel. Thus, worship is particularly crucial when one feels least like doing it.

Worship rehearses as liturgy the pattern underlying all the spirit types defining the length and breadth of the church's living. By day, by week, by year, by lifetime one is swept by the rhythm of emptying and filling and responding. Thus Christian life is the alternation of Advent as abyss, Christmas as delight, and Epiphany as mission. It is the alternation of Good Friday's contingency, within the tomb of Easter's pregnancy, for the sake of Pentecost's permeation of the world.

17. Since Christianity affirms the intersection of spirit and flesh in Incarnation as its revealing center, it is not surprising that pluralistic spirituality means living life as paradox. It means being ravished by highs and lows, implosion and explosion, silences and shoutings, freeway breadth and gates unfit for camels.

> The more spiritually developed . . . one is, the more carnal the life one lives; i.e., nothing physical or human should be alien. . . . One dances one's way through the world sleepless and trembling before its pleasures, and the unbiblical dualism between the spiritual and the material on which one may have been bred, one rightly puts down as perverse. The wine one drinks at Communion has to do with the beer one drinks downstreet. The Tersanctus one sings in chapel does not contradict the sensuousness of one's guitar. And the holy kiss of the Eucharist does not condemn the passions of one's loins and one's heart.[4]

The paradoxes of such pluralism are redeemed from derangement by incorporation into the dream of a visionary whole.

18. Spirituality, at each point, is an intimate collaboration with God. It draws one's center of gravity out of one's self toward the forward edge of things. It is strange out there, with hair free-flowing in the wind, mustering courage to refuse domestication of

the wild Spirit. It is a preposterous sanity, one that is often lonely, out there where drunks swear at closing time, owls screech in the night, and the insane howl at the moon.

Yet that is where one can lose oneself in the final Mystery, someday permanently. Until then, one is sustained by whispers on the way back. They are invitations to experience things as harbingers of a new order—promised, present, and proffered. It is a spirituality of the center, fed by stories from the edge.

> O Lord my God, thou art very great!
> Thou art clothed with honor and majesty,
>   who coverest thyself with light as with a garment,
> who hast stretched out the heavens like a tent,
>   who hast laid the beams of thy chambers on the waters, . . .
>   who ridest on the wings of the wind,
> who makest the winds thy messengers,
>   fire and flame thy ministers.
> Thou didst set the earth on its foundations,
>   so that it should never be shaken. . . .
> that [we] may bring forth food from the earth,
>   and wine to gladden the heart . . .
> oil to make [our faces] shine,
>   and bread to strengthen [our] heart. . . .
>   when thou takest away their breath, they die
>   and return to their dust.
> When thou sendest forth thy Spirit, they are created;
>   and thou renewest the face of the ground. . . .
> I will sing to the Lord as long as I live;
>   I will sing praise to my God while I have being.
>   —Psalm 104 (selected verses)

Oh, yes, one thing more:

> Blow the trumpet at the new moon,
>   at the full moon, on our feast day.
>   —Psalm 81:3

Notes

Chapter 1

1. Paul Tillich, *The Eternal Now* (New York: Charles Scribner's Sons, 1963), pp. 88–89.

2. John Macquarrie, *Paths in Spirituality* (New York: Harper & Row, 1972), p. 47.

3. John Calvin, *Institutes of the Christian Religion*, vol. XX in the Library of Christian Classics, ed. John T. McNeill (Philadelphia: Westminster Press, 1960), p. 35.

4. Frank C. Senn, ed., *Protestant Spiritual Traditions* (Mahwah, N.J.: Paulist Press, 1986), p. 4.

5. Augustine, *Confessions and Enchiridion*, trans. Albert C. Outler (Philadelphia: Westminster Press, 1953), bk. 1, ch. 1, p. 31.

6. Henri J. M. Nouwen, *Creative Ministry* (Garden City, N.Y.: Doubleday & Co., 1978), p. 88.

7. T. S. Eliot, "Four Quartets," in *The Complete Poems and Plays— 1909–1950* (New York: Harcourt, Brace & World, 1971), pp. 132–33.

Chapter 2

1. *The United Methodist Hymnal* (Nashville: The United Methodist Publishing House, 1989), hymn 88.

2. Ibid., hymn 100.

3. Ibid., hymn 103.

4. A classic expression is found in *The Cloud of Unknowing* (New York: Dell Publishing Co., 1957).

5. *The Confessions of Jacob Boehme* (New York: Harper & Brothers, 1954), pp. 46–47.

6. See Charles Hartshorne, *The Divine Relativity* (New Haven, Conn.: Yale University Press, 1948).

7. St. Hilary of Poitiers, *De Trinitate,* in *The Fathers of the Church* (New York: Fathers of the Church, Inc., 1954), vol. 25.

8. The interactive Latin term he uses is *circumincessio.* Greek thinkers at the time used the related word, *perichoresis.*

9. George Maloney, *The Mystic Light* (Denville, N.J.: Dimension Books, 1984), p. 211.

10. Merlin Stone, *When God Was a Woman* (New York: Harcourt Brace Jovanovich, 1976), p. 4.

11. Matthew Fox, *On Becoming a Musical, Mystical Bear: Spirituality American Style* (Paramus, N.J.: Paulist/Newman Press, 1972), p. 156.

12. St. Bernard of Clairvaux, *On Consideration* 5.13.27. See Ephesians 3:18.

Chapter 3

1. Abhishiktananda, *Prayer* (Philadelphia: Westminster Press, 1967), p. 29.

2. Adrian Van Kaam, *On Being Yourself* (Dimension Books), p. 53. Quoted in M. Basil Pennington, *Daily We Touch Him* (Garden City, N.Y.: Image, 1979), p. 82.

3. See Ernest Becker, *The Denial of Death* (New York: Free Press, 1973).

4. Thomas Keating, et al., *Finding Grace at the Center* (Still River, Mass.: St. Bede's Publications, 1978); Basil Pennington, *Centering Prayer* (Garden City, N.Y.: Doubleday & Co., 1980); Evelyn Underhill, *Mysticism* (New York: New American Library, 1974).

5. See William Johnston, *The Inner Eye of Love* (San Francisco: Harper & Row, 1978).

6. T. S. Eliot, "Four Quartets," in *The Complete Poems and Plays—1909–1950* (New York: Harcourt, Brace & World, 1971), p. 136.

7. Fine sources are Helen Gardner, *Art Through the Ages*, 5th ed. (New York: Harcourt, Brace & World, 1970); E. H. Gombrich, *The Story of Art* (New York: Phaidon Publishers, 1950); John Canaday, *Metropolitan Seminars in Art* (New York: The Metropolitan Museum of Art, 1960).

8. For readers interested in painting as applied to this spirit type, worth consulting are: Nolde's ominous quality of the limitlessness in *Heavy Seas at Sunset* and *Evening on the Langenese;* the abyss hinted in

each center, as in de Martini's *Moonlight;* the bold power of over-againstness in Rousseau's *The Equatorial Jungle;* or the nature mysticism of Friedrich's *Cloister Graveyard in the Snow,* or *Landscape in the Silesian Mountains.*

9. Miriam Arguelles and Jose Arguelles, *The Feminine: Spacious as the Sky* (Boulder, Colo.: Shambhala Publications, 1977), p. 6.

Chapter 4

1. *The United Methodist Hymnal* (Nashville: The United Methodist Publishing House, 1989), hymn 103.

2. *The Way of the Pilgrim* (New York: Ballantine Books, 1974).

3. See Vernard Eller, *The Simple Life: The Christian Stance Toward Possessions* (Grand Rapids: Wm. B. Eerdmans Publishing Co., 1973); Richard Foster, *Freedom of Simplicity* (San Francisco: Harper & Row, 1981).

4. Other paintings worth consulting for this spirit type include Mondrian's gradual abstraction of trees into the pure form of color, space, and line, as life's simplest forms to be experienced for their own sake (for example, *Opposition of Lines,* and *Red and Yellow*). Also Seurat's peaceful order of the inviolate in *The Side Show.* Also worth considering is Modigliani's timeless and sober order hinting of an eternalized integrity (e.g., *Seated Nude*), and Feininger's transparent layers of inward form and depth, as in *Blue Cloud.*

Chapter 5

1. Fritjof Capra, *Tao of Physics* (New York: Bantam Books, 1984).

2. St. John of the Cross, "Poetry," in *The Collected Works of St. John of the Cross* (Washington, D.C.: Institute of Carmelite Studies, 1979), pp. 711–37.

3. Herman Melville, *Moby Dick* (New York: Modern Library, 1950), p. 2.

4. Ibid., p. 3.

5. From a Sermon on Psalm 41 addressed to the newly baptized by Jerome.

6. See *Say Amen, Somebody,* record from soundtrack, DRE Records, Inc., 157 W. 57th St., New York, NY 10019. Produced and directed by George T. Nierenberg.

7. Other paintings conducive to this spirit type include the musiclike orchestrations of Kandinsky, as in *Improvisation 33 for Orient.* Or in Rothko's fantasy play with color, as *No. 8.* And the lively fascination with pure energy in almost any of Turner's later work.

Chapter 6

1. One of the most powerful single affirmations of this mode appears in the sermon "You Are Accepted," in Paul Tillich, *Shaking the Foundations* (New York: Charles Scribners' Sons, 1952), chap. 19, pp. 153–63.

2. George A. Maloney, *Inward Stillness* (Denville, N.J.: Dimension Books, 1976), p. 57.

3. Karl Barth, *Church Dogmatics* (London: T. & T. Clark, 1960), vol. 3, pt. 3, pp. 224–25.

4. David Knight, "Desert Spirituality—An Answer to Massah and Meribah," *Studies in Formative Spirituality* 1, no. 2 (May 1980): 181–92.

5. Charles Cummings, "Job's Desert Experience," *Studies in Formative Spirituality* 1, no. 2 (May 1980): 227–36.

6. Henry Thoreau, *Walden*, in *The Portable Thoreau*, ed. Carl Bode (New York: Viking Press, 1947); see especially "Where I Lived, and What I Lived For," pp. 334ff. For a current option, see *Poustinia* (Notre Dame, Ind.: Ave Maria Press, 1974).

7. Ed Hayes, *Prayers for the Domestic Church* (Easton, Kan.: Shantivanam House of Prayer, 1979), pp. 119–28; John Michael Talbot, *Hermitage* (New York: Crossroad, 1989).

8. See Alan Jones, *Soul Making* (San Francisco: Harper & Row, 1985). See also Benedicta Ward, *The Desert Christian* (New York: Macmillan Publishing Co.).

9. T. S. Eliot, *The Waste Land and Other Poems* (New York: Harcourt, Brace & Co., 1930), p. 30.

10. *Christian Prayer: The Liturgy of the Hours* (Boston: Daughters of St. Paul, 1976).

11. Other paintings suggesting spirit type 4 are Munch's *The Cry*, with its pervading terror yet ominous fascination in the disquieting. In the uncanny, bewitched fabric of Chirico's work, as in *The Anguish of Departure*, appears a panicky anxiety, a foreboding space, a disturbed time, a haunted silence coating anything that exists. Also worth considering is the profound pathos of professed self-sufficiency in Toulouse-Lautrec's *At the Moulin Rouge* or the lurking frailty of Degas's *Woman with Chrysanthemums*.

12. *The Sacramentary* (New York: Catholic Book Publishing Co., 1974), p. 1011.

13. John Wesley, "Watchnight Service," in *The Book of Worship for Church and Home* (Nashville: The Methodist Publishing House, 1964), p. 387.

Chapter 7

1. Joachim Jeremias, *The Lord's Prayer* (Philadelphia: Fortress Press, 1964); Joachim Jeremias, *The Prayers of Jesus* (Philadelphia: Fortress Press, 1978).

2. T. S. Eliot, "Four Quartets," in *The Complete Poems and Plays—1909–1950* (New York: Harcourt, Brace & World, 1971), p. 44.

3. Brother Lawrence, *The Practice of the Presence of God* (Springfield, Ill.: Templegate, 1974), p. 29 and passim.

4. P. T. Forsythe, *The Soul of Prayer* (Grand Rapids: Wm. B. Eerdmans Publishing Co., 1916), p. 92. See pp. 81–92.

5. For help in this, read Walter Wink, *Transforming Bible Study* (Nashville: Abingdon Press, 1980).

6. See Carolyn Stahl, *Opening to God* (Nashville: Upper Room, 1977).

7. Quoted by Canon Etienne Ledeur, "The Spiritual Tradition," in *Imitating Christ* (St. Meinrad, Ind.: Abbey Press, 1974), p. 62.

8. Ibid., p. 64.

9. Charles M. Sheldon, *In His Steps* (New York: Permabooks, 1949).

10. Amos Wilder, *The Language of the Gospel, Early Christian Rhetoric* (Harper & Row, 1964), p. 67.

11. Georges Bernanos, *Diary of a Country Priest* (Garden City, N.Y.: Doubleday & Co., 1954). Nikos Kazantzakis, *The Last Temptation of Christ* (New York: Bantam Books, 1960).

12. For example, Gabriel Fackre, *The Christian Story* (Grand Rapids: Wm. B. Eerdmans Publishing Co., 1984).

13. The "secular" version of this spirit type appears in Daumier's work, where finitude is rendered intolerable unless it is the habitat of spirit. This interiority of redemptive power appears as compassion in such works as *Jugglers at Rest, The Third-Class Carriage, Don Quixote,* and *The Washerwoman.* His is the ability to recognize innate worth as an alien gift, hinting of an abiding divinity at the heart of shopworn weariness.

14. Lawrence, *Practice of the Presence,* p. 29 and passim.

15. Albert Camus, *The Myth of Sisyphus* (New York: Vintage Books, 1959), p. 13.

Chapter 8

1. Robert Frost, "The Road Not Taken," in *Robert Frost's Poems,* ed. Louis Untermeyer (New York: Washington Square Press, 1946), p. 223.

2. Francis Thompson, "The Hound of Heaven," in *A Little Treasury*

of Modern Poetry, ed. Oscar Williams (New York: Charles Scribner's Sons, 1952), pp. 601–02.

3. Ibid., p. 603.

4. George F. Simons, *Keeping Your Personal Journal* (New York: Paulist Press, 1978); Ronald Klug, *How to Keep a Spiritual Journal* (New York: Thomas Nelson Publishers, 1982); Harry J. Cargas, *Keeping a Spiritual Journal* (Garden City, N.Y.: Doubleday & Co., 1981); Ira Progoff, *At a Journal Workshop* (New York: Dialogue House, 1977). See May Sarton, *Journal of a Solitude* (New York: W. W. Norton & Co., 1973).

5. *The Book of Worship for Church and Home* (Nashville: The Methodist Publishing House, 1964), pp. 382–88.

6. Fascinating reading here is C. G. Jung, *Memories, Dreams, Reflections* (New York: Pantheon Books, 1973).

7. Kathryn Lindskoog, *The Gift of Dreams* (San Francisco: Harper & Row, 1979); Morton Kelsey, *Dreams: A Way to Listen to God* (New York: Paulist Press, 1978).

8. Dennis Linn and Matthew Linn, *Healing Life's Hurts* (New York: Paulist Press, 1977); Dennis Linn and Matthew Linn, *Healing of Memories* (Paramus, N.J.: Paulist/Newman Press, 1974); Ruth C. Stapleton, *The Gift of Inner Healing* (Waco, Tex.: Word Books, 1977); Morton Kelsey, *Healing and Christianity* (San Francisco: Harper & Row, 1973); Frances MacNutt, *Power to Heal* (Notre Dame, Ind.: Ave Maria Press, 1977); Agnes Sanford, *The Healing Light* (New York: Paulist Press, 1977).

9. Tony Stoneburner, ed., *Parable, Myth, and Language* (Cambridge: Church Society for College Work, 1968), p. 68.

10. This inventory can be taken in a shortened form in D. Kiersey and M. Bates, *Please Understand Me* (Del Mar, Calif.: Prometheus Books, 1978); W. Harold Grant et al., *From Image to Likeness: A Jungian Path in the Gospel Journey* (Ramsey, N.J.: Paulist Press, 1983); Chester P. Michael, and Marie C. Norrisey, *Prayer and Temperament* (Charlottesville, Va.: Open Door, 1984).

11. Other paintings illustrative of this spirit type include: Botticelli's *The Birth of Venus;* Rouault's *The Old King* or *Afterglow;* Soutine's *The Choirboy.*

12. T. S. Eliot, *The Waste Land*, p. 46.

Chapter 9

1. Johan Huizinga, *Homo Ludens* (Boston: Beacon Press, 1950), pp. 212–13.

2. *Collected Letters: St. Thérèse of Lisieux* (London: Sheed & Ward, 1949), p. 13.

4. Tilden Edwards, *Sabbath Time* (New York: Seabury Press, 1982).

5. Robin Maas and Gabriel O'Donnell, *Spiritual Traditions for the Contemporary Church* (Nashville: Abingdon Press, 1990), p. 46.

6. I find useful the lectionary readings called the "American Ordo" of the Roman Catholic Church, sent monthly by request from the Priests of the Sacred Heart, P.O. Box 900, Hales Corners, WI 53130.

7. Heribert Muhlen, *Charismatic Theology: Initiation in the Spirit* (New York: Paulist Press, 1978); John Sherrill, *They Speak in Other Tongues* (Old Tappan, N.J.: Fleming H. Revell Co., 1966).

8. One can sense this spirit type in the shimmering surface texture of Renoir's *Girl with Basket of Fish*. Or in Chagall's work, where dream and reality frolic innocently together, as in *I and the Village*. Or consider the playful symbols of Miró's *Man, Woman, and Child*, and the primordial innocence of soul in Makovsky's *Children with Japanese Lanterns*.

Chapter 10

1. Martin Buber, *I and Thou* (Edinburgh: T. & T. Clark, 1937), pp. 7ff.

2. Lawrence LeShan, *How to Meditate* (Boston: Little, Brown & Co., 1974), p. 36.

3. See, for example, the eight chant modes developed from Gregorian chant by St. Meinrad's Seminary, St. Meinrad, Indiana.

4. The Ven. Chao Khun Phra Tepsiddhimuni Mahathera, *The Path to Nibbana* (Vipassana Center, Sect. 5, Mahadhatu Monastery, Bangkok 2, Thailand).

5. Rainer Maria Rilke, *Duino Elegies*, in *Selected Works: Poetry* (New York: New Directions Publishing Corp.), "The Eighth Elegy."

6. One can find further expressions of this spirit type in Chardin, where each object has a rare solemnity, for example, *The Blessing* or *The Kitchen Maid*. In Gauguin the sacramental takes on the direct impact of earth symbols, as in *Two Tahitian Women with Mangoes*. In Wood and Benton, events natural and historic take on the power of parable. And with Wyeth, even an empty plate and saucer on an old table before an open window convey the stark hint of Eucharist.

7. Thomas Merton, *New Seeds of Contemplation* (New York: New Directions Publishing Corp., 1961), pp. 296–297.

Chapter 11

1. Thomas Merton, *New Seeds*, p. 210.

2. *The Sacramentary* (New York: Catholic Book Publishing Co., 1974); see, for example, p. 560.

3. *The Collected Works of St. John of The Cross* (Washington, D.C.:

Institute of Carmelite Studies, 1979), p. 714.

4. Augustine, *Tractates on the First Letter of John*, Tract. 4: PL 35: 2008, in *Christian Prayer: The Liturgy of the Hours* (Boston: Daughters of St. Paul, 1976), pp. 1706–07.

5. Parker Palmer, *To Know as We Are Known* (New York: Harper & Row, 1983), pp. 82–83.

6. Richard J. Foster, *Celebration of Discipline* (San Francisco: Harper & Row, 1978), pp. 150ff.

7. See Jacques Guillet et al., *Discernment of Spirits* (Collegeville, Minn.: Liturgical Press, 1981); John Carroll Futrell, S.J., "Ignatian Discernment," in *Studies in the Spirituality of Jesuits*, vol. 2, no. 2 (April 1970); Futrell, "Common Discernment: Reflections on Experience," in *Studies in the Spirituality of Jesuits*, vol. 4, no. 5 (November 1972); Jean Laplace, *Preparing for Spiritual Direction* (Chicago: Franciscan Herald Press, 1975); William J. Connolly, S.J., "Contemporary Spiritual Direction: Scope and Principles," in *Studies in the Spirituality of Jesuits*, vol. 7, no. 3 (June 1975).

8. For example, *R.B. 1980: The Rule of St. Benedict*, in Latin and English with Notes (Collegeville, Minn.: Liturgical Press, 1981).

9. Thomas Oden, *Care of Souls in the Classic Tradition* (Philadelphia: Fortress Press, 1984), p. 18.

10. Tilden Edwards, *Spiritual Friend* (New York: Paulist Press, 1980); Kenneth Leech, *Soul Friend* (London: Sheldon Press, 1977); William A. Barry and William J. Connolly, *The Practice of Spiritual Direction* (San Francisco: Harper & Row, 1982); Alan Jones, *Exploring Spiritual Direction* (New York: Harper & Row, 1989).

11. David Watkins, *Accountable Discipleship* (Nashville: Discipleship Resources, 1984). Dietrich Bonhoeffer, *Life Together* (New York: Harper & Brothers, 1954).

12. Gustavo Gutiérrez, *We Drink from Our Own Wells* (Maryknoll, N.Y.: Orbis Books, 1984).

13. *Newsweek*, September 4, 1989, p. 56.

Chapter 12

1. Walter J. Lowe, "Against Experience: Reflections on Theology and the Devotional Life." Unpublished manuscript.

2. Ibid.

3. Eliot, "Four Quartets," in *The Complete Poems and Plays*, p. 44.

4. *Voyage, Vision, Venture*, "Report of the Task Force on Spiritual Development" (Dayton, Ohio: American Association of Theological Schools, 1972), p. 23. I have taken the liberty of making the personal pronouns inclusive.